GOD'S TRUTH ABOUT GENDER

Unraveling the Lies of Modern Human Sexuality, Behavior, and Identity

Dr. David E. James IV

VMI Publishers • Sisters, Oregon

Dedication

This book is dedicated to my late uncle.

The spirit of my uncle was fierce. He loved lions. He always had a symbol of a lion somewhere around. To him, the lion symbolized strength, power, dominion, principle and purpose. He lived based on these principles. He saw himself as capable. He was a capable father, husband, uncle, athlete, friend, mentor and any other role that he required of himself to fill. He taught me many principles of what it means to be a man.

He led by example. He not only shared with me his successes in life, but he shared with me his fears and failures as well. This made him real in my eyes. I did not have to pretend around him. He taught me that I did not have to be perfect, but I should never settle for less than what I require of myself. In the end, I should always require that which God requires of me.

His lion's heart is what I will remember the most and what I will miss about him the most. His spirit and legacy will live in me and the others to whom he imparted his wisdom, knowledge and strength. Thanks for sharing yourself and your life with me. I will always do my best to live up to your example. You are a true warrior [armor bearer], a lion in every sense of the word.

God's Truth about Gender © 2008 by David E. James
All rights reserved.

Unless otherwise indicated, Scripture references are taken from the *Holy Bible, New International Version* Copyright © 1973, 1978, 1984 by International Bible Society. Used by permission of Zondervan Bible Publishers.

Scripture marked KJV is taken from the *King James Version* of the Bible.

Due to the personal and sensitive nature of the material in this book, the author has chosen to use a pseudonym. All of the author's medical qualifications and personal experiences are true.

Published by
VMI Publishers
Sisters, Oregon
www.vmipublishers.com

ISBN: 1-933204-60-5
ISBN 13: 978-1-933204-60-4
Library of Congress Control Number: 2008927918

Printed in the USA.

Contents and/or cover may not be reproduced in part or in whole without the expressed written consent of the Publisher.

Cover design by Joe Bailen

Table of Contents

Introduction 9

CHAPTER ONE: PARALLEL WORLDS 19
    The Duality of Man 19
    The Fall of Man 24
    The Concept of Parallel Worlds 27

CHAPTER TWO: SEXUAL SINS 31

CHAPTER THREE: THE POWER OF LOVE 37

CHAPTER FOUR: HUMAN DEVELOPMENT (Spiritual and Physical) 45
    Modeled Behavior (Spiritual) 45
    The Physiology of Behavior (Physical)
        —Neuroplasticity and Addiction 48

CHAPTER FIVE: BEHOLD THE IMAGE 55
    Gender 55
    The Qualities of Gender 59

CHAPTER SIX: SEX, MARRIAGE, AND OBEDIENCE 61

CHAPTER SEVEN: CRISIS OF IDENTITY 69
    Gender and Identity 69
    Sexuality and Choice 71

CHAPTER EIGHT: HOMOSEXUALITY AND GENDER BALANCE 77
    Male Homosexuality 77
    Female Homosexuality 85
    Balanced Genders 86

CHAPTER NINE: THE FATHER 89

CHAPTER TEN: STRENGTH OF THE FEMININE 97

CHAPTER ELEVEN: GENDER INTERDEPENDENCE 105
    The Balance of God 105
    Eve's Fear 108

CHAPTER TWELVE: AN EQUAL OFFERING TO GIVE 111
    Honoring the Masculine 111
    Honoring the Feminine 112

CHAPTER THIRTEEN: THE HOMOSEXUAL
   AND TRANSGENDERED MIND 115

CHAPTER FOURTEEN: THE HEART OF MAN—
   SEAT OF THE SOUL, COMMANDER OF THE WILL 121

CHAPTER FIFTEEN: THE HEALING OF MAN 133
    Love Wounds 133
    The Matrix (Denial and Repression) 135
    Femininity, Mercy, and Forgiveness 143

CHAPTER SIXTEEN: BATTLE OF THE MIND 147
    Polarity, Choice, and Sin 147
    The Weapons of War 150

CHAPTER SEVENTEEN: A STORY OF PERSONAL AWAKENING 157

BIBLIOGRAPHY 207

Acknowledgments

To my wife, Varee. Your God-like faithfulness toward me is beyond measure. You completely embody the feminine image of our Lord in a way that is difficult to find in the earth today. I am truly in awe of you, for you are a woman, fearfully and wonderfully made. In you I have been witness to the alluring beauty, comforting desire, fidelity, and mercy of God given to the world in women. As Eve was to Adam a gift from God, so have you been God's undeserved gift to me from the first day I met you. Thank you for loving me and being an anchor in my life. You are the image of our God that, in feminine glue-like strength, holds our family together by faithfulness, servitude, humility, dedication, and unwavering obedience to God. I am blessed beyond that of many men in the earth today, for a virtuous wife of your caliber is a rare find indeed.

> A wife of noble character who can find? She is worth far more than rubies. Her husband has full confidence in her and lacks nothing of value. She brings him good, not harm, all the days of her life. Many women do noble things, but you surpass them all.
>
> Proverbs 31:10–12, 29

To my daughter Mona, trust in God always and hold on to your feminine heart as you learn about the freeing power of forgiveness. Use forgiveness as a defensive weapon. It will shield you against those who, in confusion and pain, have left their scars upon your heart. To my daughter Mariah, you are my "little feminine," precious beyond belief. To my son, David, I see in you my past and my future. You are my pride and joy. May you grow in the masculine strength and image of our God.

Introduction

The fool says in his heart, 'There is no God'" (Psalm 14:1). The basis of this book rests on one premise: that God is and has been from the beginning; He created humankind (male and female); He created us with purpose and without accident. This must be believed by faith, as it can never be proven. An inventor invents a work for a purpose, and its purpose shows forth in the intelligence of its design. God is our master builder, creator, and inventor. Our purpose, though obscure at times, shows forth in the beauty and intelligence of our design.

> For since the creation of the world God's invisible qualities—his eternal power and divine nature—have been clearly seen, being understood from what has been made, so that men are without excuse.
>
> ROMANS 1:20

This is the word that came to Jeremiah from the Lord: "Go down to the potter's house, and there I will give you my message." So I went down to the potter's house, and I saw him working at the wheel. But the pot he was shaping from the clay was marred in his hands; so the potter formed it into another pot, shaping it as seemed best to him. Then the word of the Lord came to me: "O house of Israel, can I not do with you as this potter does?" declares the Lord. "Like clay in the hand of the potter, so are you in my hand."

JEREMIAH 18:1–6

This book is breathed from the mouth of God through a vessel of clay (me) who has willingly humbled himself under the hands of the master builder. In obedience I have chosen to speak the words that God has chosen to release into the earth at this time. This is essentially the role of a prophet. A prophet is a chosen vessel of God who has been given a word or message intended for a particular group of people. It is not the role of a prophet to be concerned with the response of any individual to the spoken word. Whether an individual hears the word, understands it, and then, as an act of the will, chooses behavior consistent with the word, is a matter of receptivity to God, not the prophet.

"Son of man, I have made you a watchman for the house of Israel; so hear the word I speak and give them warning from me. When I say to a wicked man, 'You will surely die,' and you do not warn him or speak out to dissuade him from his evil ways in order to save his life, that wicked man will die for his sin, and I will hold you accountable for his blood. But if you do warn the wicked man and he does not turn from his wickedness or from his evil ways, he will die for his sin; but you will have saved yourself.

"But when I speak to you, I will open your mouth and you shall say to them, 'This is what the Sovereign Lord says.' Whoever will listen let him listen, and whoever will refuse let him refuse.

"Son of man, I am sending you to the Israelites, to a rebellious nation that has rebelled against me; they and their fathers have been in revolt against me to this very day. The people to whom I am sending you are obstinate and stubborn...

> "And whether they listen or fail to listen—for they are a rebellious house—they will know that a prophet has been among them.
>
> "But you, son of man, listen to what I say to you. Do not rebel like that rebellious house; open your mouth and eat what I give you."
>
> Then I looked, and I saw a hand stretched out to me. In it was a scroll, which he unrolled before me. On both sides of it were written words of lament and mourning and woe.
>
> And he said to me, "Son of man, eat what is before you, eat this scroll; then go and speak to the house of Israel."
>
> EZEKIEL 3:17–19, 27; 2:3–5, 8–10; 3:1

God is always communicating with us. However, many times the individuals whom God intends to communicate with are incapable of hearing directly from Him in a spiritual sense. This could be due to a multitude of reasons; for instance, involvement in sin or lack of belief, faith, or understanding of the ways in which He speaks to us humans.

When God speaks, He always speaks to the spirit. By this I mean that God is concerned with truth of existence, purpose, behavior, and the realities of spiritual life such as fear, faith, truth, lies, obedience, rebellion, fidelity, adultery, good, and evil. These are not things we can touch or feel in the physical but are nevertheless as real as any physical object. This is the realm of the spirit, and this is where we find God, always.

Man has become physically/earthly focused as a result of our spiritual death and departure from God due to sin. We find ourselves concerned mainly with issues of concrete physical realities, things we can see, touch, taste, hear, smell, etc., the natural senses.

Science has become the god of man, separated from a spiritual God who is not primarily found in the physical, though we can see His handiwork all over the physically created universe. We were not created to exist in this way alone. When we try to use science as an avenue to explain our existence as spiritual beings, we show our disconnect from God.

Spiritual existence is concerned with issues of belief, purpose, morality, and behavior. These are not physical realities but spiritual ones. Science will never explain why a lie is wrong and the truth is right. It cannot speak to the concept of rightness or wrongness. Morality is not a scientific construct, but a spiritual one. Therefore, to try to explain moral issues of behavior by scientific methods leaves an individual without the tools to accomplish the desired task.

Science and religion speak to two separate realities of human existence: the natural and the spiritual, respectively. To hold one in higher esteem and ignore the other shows a form of human misunderstanding. Spiritual and physical realities mirror one another in creation. What is true spiritually will find its order in the physical universe as well.

Contrary to the prevailing belief of many, science and religion are not at odds with each other. They are merely two avenues by which we understand creation. We use either science or religion/spiritual understanding to answer questions regarding the issues at hand. If one wants to understand the human, biological physiology behind chemical dependency and substance-abuse issues, he must consult science, for this is a well-documented phenomenon of human existence. If one wants to know whether it is right or wrong that an individual becomes or stays addicted, he must consult religion/spirituality, for with this question he has crossed over from the physical to the realm of morality.

Physiology has nothing to do with morality, except in the sense that morality gives meaning to it. Even when not under the influence of their chosen drug, chemical addicts are plagued by a physical condition that hinders their ability to make appropriate choices based on their personal beliefs and moral judgments. They are biologically, chemically, organically, and physically restrained, not free agents of their own will. This is, in essence, a form of slavery, albeit a condition from within the individual, not from without, as in the human slavery that marks US history.

With this understanding, we can see how religion rises to the task of communicating moral reasoning to the behavioral issues surrounding chemical and drug addiction, something physiology does not even begin to address. It is one thing to understand the concept of slavery, but quite another to understand it to be wrong. The following quote is taken from a book that is coauthored by two individuals, Stanton L. Jones and Mark A.

Yarhouse. It contrasts the ways in which science and spirituality/religion offer understanding to what we know to be true.

> We believe that both religious faith and science deal with reality. Although they deal with differing slices of reality, these slices are overlapping. If this claim is true, it would suggest that both religious belief and science are likely to be important and informative in our understanding of human life. Science deals with aspects of reality that we can measure, repeat and manipulate (these are what we refer to as empirical aspects of reality). Science measures certain events, phenomena and experiences, and reports on what it finds within the limitations of scientific methods of inquiry.
>
> But what about religious faith? Like the apostle Paul we believe that Christianity is about two primary sorts of "things": God's acts in the world and God's Word. His acts are events that are historical realities and hence empirical realities of a sort, even if those historical realities cannot be controlled and repeated by the scientist.
>
> God's Word is the historical self-revelation in human language from the eternal God of the universe. This linguistic self-revelation makes claims about what is true—claims to which we must respond. If these historic events are fabrications, and if these knowledge claims in God's Word are false, then we are above all people to be pitied because we are deluded.[1]

We are primarily spiritual beings, given physical bodies in which to rule the earth as kings and queens bearing the spiritual image of our Creator, who is spirit. To lose sight of our spiritual existence, which connects us to God, means to lose understanding of our true reality and our purpose for creation. In this manner we lose our understanding of God, for He is not physical but spirit. We then become fools, because apart from connection to God and purpose we are no different from animals in regard to behavior and moral existence.

Many issues will be touched upon in this text, including marriage, sexuality, parenting, psychology, human development, behavior, and addiction.

With an appropriate degree of self-analysis, you should be able to tackle with some certainty whatever God may reveal as you read the material presented. As you forge through the information, you may find that certain information does not apply directly to your present situation. This is okay. You can glean valuable insight into God's dealings with mankind through understanding how human nature goes bad under myriad circumstances.

Be humble as a reader and you will receive the personal message God wishes to communicate to you. Don't be too quick to conclude that something does not personally apply to you. You may be dismissing valuable information God wants to show you about your own existence or that of a loved one.

This book must be read from beginning to end in its entirety in order to receive the complete message intended for the reader to obtain. Many of the topics spoken of early on will be imperative to the understanding of the remaining chapters. The early chapters serve as foundational material essential to the complete picture intended to be revealed by the book as a whole. To read it out of sequence would deal a fatal blow to the message and leave you no more enlightened than if you had never read it.

A certain amount of maturity is needed to follow instruction, persevere, and not hastily read past valuable information. A great degree of maturity will also be needed in self-analysis and introspection, which will serve as the vehicle through which this information will ultimately make its abode in your heart, thereby producing the possibility of change.

Because of this criteria, many will not receive the message in the way it is intended. Nevertheless, whether you grasp and receive this message is ultimately a matter between you and God. I can only, in obedience, write the words that have been given to me. I stand before God as an obedient prophet. I make no attempt to change the message for political purposes or fear of offense to certain individuals.

This will not be an easy message to swallow for many. If this is true for you, your argument is with God, not me. It is not the goal of this book to argue with individuals who have chosen darkness over light. Their hearts are such that truth cannot penetrate. If this is the case with you, this book is not meant for you. He who will hear, let him hear; and he who will reject, let him reject.

> For this people's heart has become calloused; they hardly hear with their ears, and they have closed their eyes. Otherwise they might see with their eyes, hear with their ears, understand with their hearts and turn, and I would heal them.
>
> MATTHEW 13:15

If this is not your situation, you are a blessed individual, because with this book the possibility of spiritual healing has now become available to you. Amen.

Revelation is the method by which God gives man knowledge about Himself and His creation that he could not have otherwise known. All knowledge about human existence and behavior is rooted in God. He holds the key to true understanding. Any school of thought or practice that excludes or contradicts the revealed knowledge of God is folly. For if truth is rooted in God and has already been revealed in His Word, what can the former be but error?

The Diagnostics and Statistical Manual of Mental Disorders (DSM) lists different categories of mental disorders and the criteria for their diagnosis. There have been five major revisions since it was first published in 1952. Published by the American Psychiatric Association, it is the primary tool used by mental-health professionals in practice today. In 1973 homosexuality was removed from the DSM III as a mental illness. This decision was not based on popular professional consensus, but on political pressure from a special-interest group then in its infancy: the gay rights movement. To this day this political coup is touted as proof that modern psychology has embraced homosexuality as a normal variant to human sexuality. This is believed despite decades of studies that consistently indicate otherwise.

> The decision to drop homosexuality as disorder ignores the large body of accumulated literature indicating psychodynamic connections between unresolved and largely unconscious conflicts and homosexual orientation. This literature, wrought from clinical experience, sees homosexuality as a sexualized resolution of conflict in

which the particular traumatizing experiences of an individual became interwoven with psychosexual development.

Despite the official position of the APA duly confirmed by a membership vote, a significant number of psychiatrists did not agree with it. A survey taken four years after the APA decision by the journal *Medical Aspects of Human Sexuality* found that 69 percent of responding psychiatrists agreed that "homosexuality is usually a pathological adaptation, as opposed to a normal variation."

As of 1995, the membership in NARTH, the National Association for Research and Treatment of Homosexuality, numbered 425 mental health professionals. NARTH, founded only in 1992, is composed mostly of accredited therapists who work with homosexual persons distressed by their condition and seeking change toward heterosexual functioning.[2]

Contrary to what is frequently and erroneously stated in the media, there is no scientific or psychological proof that homosexuality is anything other than a behavior pattern that manifests itself in certain individuals for a variety of reasons, including psychological, social, environmental, behavioral, and genetic predispositions working together to produce the homosexual persona.

Regardless of how or why the decision was made to treat homosexuality as a normal variant to human behavior patterns, this lifestyle is in direct contradiction to the Scriptures, which are clear regarding the departure of homosexual behavior from normal, God-sanctioned human sexuality.

Psychologists, to be wise, must have their roots in the already revealed truths of human existence, much of which is found in biblical teachings. Otherwise, they become fools and their teachings false; their ability to heal the psyche, lost; their council, misleading; the validity of their trade, void. To leave God in any form is to fall into the uttermost darkness, for He is our Creator and holds all that is needed for health, healing, and wholeness.

All Scripture is God-breathed and is useful for teaching, rebuking, correcting and training in righteousness, so that the man of God may be thoroughly equipped for every good work.

2 Timothy 3:16–17

For although they knew God, they neither glorified him as God nor gave thanks to him, but their thinking became futile and their foolish hearts were darkened. Although they claimed to be wise, they became fools.

Romans 1:21–22

The secret things belong to the Lord our God, but the things revealed belong to us and to our children forever, that we may follow all the words of this law.

Deuteronomy 29:29

In the end, God's truth stands as a banner for any who would seek wholeness and balm for the weary soul. His Word sets the foundation for the healing of humankind concerning whatever is amiss in our lives. "He sent his word, and healed them, and delivered them from their destructions" (Psalm 107:20 KJV). "Sanctify them by the truth; your word is truth" (John 17:17).

---

[1]Stanton L. Jones and Mark A. Yarhouse, *Homosexuality: The Use of Scientific Research in the Church's Moral Debate* (InterVarsity Press, 2000).
[2]John F. Harvey, *The Truth about Homosexuality* (Ignatius Press, 1996).

CHAPTER ONE

Parallel Worlds
(Spiritual/Natural)

The Duality of Man

One of the premises of this book is that God created all things. This includes the spiritual elements of the universe as well as the physical elements. He created angels that dwell in the spiritual realm, and he created animals that dwell in the physical/earthly realm. God and angels are spiritual beings. Animals and other forms of matter (earth, sun, stars, etc.) are natural forms of creation that abide by the laws of physics; e.g., gravity. But what about man?

The biggest thing that separates man from all other forms of created life is the fact that God created man in His image. What does it mean to be created in the image of God? The answer to this question is multidimensional. We will deal with all the facets of this question later in the book. However, at this point, it must be pointed out that part of what it means to be created in the image of God is to possess an existence that is likened unto His existence, which takes on spiritual form. Man must and does possess a spiritual existence analogous to that of God, angels, and other personalities of the spirit world. This is the main difference between man and other forms of created life in the natural.

> Then God said, "Let us make man in our image, in our likeness."
> So God created man in his own image, in the image of God he created him; male and female he created them. The Lord God formed the man from the dust of the ground and breathed into his nostrils the breath of life, and the man became a living being.
>
> GENESIS 1:26—27; 2:7

With man, a distinction was made. God did not reveal the breathing of life in regard to other forms in creation. Nor did He call them living beings. Nor did He say, "Let us make animals in our image." All of these qualities were spoken over man alone in reference to creation.

I believe man also stands apart from the spiritually created beings in that we possess dual natures: spirit and natural. The following Scripture describes the natural state of humankind:

> By the sweat of your brow you will eat your food until you return to the ground, since from it you were taken; for dust you are and to dust you will return.
> So the Lord God banished him from the Garden of Eden to work the ground from which he had been taken. After he drove the man out, he placed on the east side of the Garden of Eden cherubim and a flaming sword flashing back and forth to guard the way to the tree of life.
>
> GENESIS 3:19, 23—24

It has not been revealed that angels, demons, cherubim, etc. have been formed from dust. They are spiritual beings and abide by the laws of the spiritual realm. God was and always has been. He is spirit. And so it is that I make my premise that man possesses dual natures: natural and spiritual. Subsequently, man must function and exist in relationship to the laws that govern both the natural and spiritual realms. The laws that govern the natural are evident; for example, laws of energy, entropy, thermodynamics, Newton's three laws of motion. But the laws that govern the spiritual universe are not as evident to those who are dead (blind) to the spirit. These polar spiritual laws have positive/good and negative/bad connotations. They are as follows:

Faith vs. fear

Forgiveness vs. guilt/shame/blame (Guilt/shame and blame are the same, different only in the perspective from which unforgiveness comes. If from oneself, it is guilt/shame; from another it is blame).

Truth vs. lie. "I do not write to you because you do not know the truth, but because you do know it and because no lie comes from the truth" (1 John 2:21).

Hope vs. doubt

Obedience vs. rebellion (disobedience)

Fidelity vs. adultery (spiritual and natural concepts). In the spirit, I speak of fidelity in reference to a perpetual cleaving to a promise regardless of circumstance. Adultery means to choose another alliance from that of a previously promised covenant. It is typically done sporadically, as in a wavering commitment. In the natural, fidelity and adultery are in reference to sexual practices understood in light of the marriage covenant.

Cleanliness (pure/holy) vs. uncleanliness (impure/unholy). "Who can bring what is pure from the impure? No one!" (Job 14:4).

Marriage vs. divorce (spiritual and natural concepts). In the spirit, marriage is a concept that embodies all spiritual laws on the positive poles of spirituality. It is a commitment to always behave in all of these ways in reference to another person. It is always a choice. Spiritual divorce is a choice to behave otherwise. Spiritual divorce is similar to spiritual adultery in that it is the ultimate adulterous choice. It is not a sporadic failure of commitment, as in adultery. It is a choice to be done with completely, totally forsaking a previous promise of commitment.

Sacrifice vs. selfishness

Humility vs. pride

Light vs. darkness (spiritual and natural concepts). Spiritual light is the ability to see truth and understand spiritual concepts. Darkness is blind to spiritual understanding and truth.

Good vs. evil

Life vs. death (spiritual and natural concepts). Spiritual life is similar to spiritual marriage in that it entails all behaviors on the positive spiritual pole, albeit not necessarily related to a covenant or promise to another individual. You can be alive or dead to any particular concept or personality. In regard to concepts, divorce is the death of a marriage. Interpersonally, selfishness is the death of sacrifice, rebellion is the death of obedience, adultery is the death of fidelity, blame/guilt/shame is the death of forgiveness.

As it is in the natural, there is polarity in the spiritual world. We know temperature (hot and cold), direction (up and down, left and right), color (black and white), size (big and small), weight, which is a function of gravity (heavy and light), etc. In the natural, you cannot draw closer to hot without moving farther away from cold. In the spirit, you cannot draw closer to the truth without moving further away from a lie.

These spiritual laws are not natural and are impossible to comprehend by those who deny their spiritual connection to God. As we exist in the natural and are controlled by the forces of gravity seemingly without notice, we are also moved by spiritual laws apparently without notice.

All people, whether they admit it or not, have a God conscience. We inherently know that lying is bad and telling the truth is good. We speak of right and wrong in our daily lives. We hold a belief system that in itself implies real and not real or truth and non-truth. The fact that we do this unconsciously gives insight into our connection with the intangible.

This is the realm of morality that ceases to exist apart from the laws that govern the spiritual world. Some may claim to not believe in morality. They live as if they are animals, one preying upon the other with seemingly no guilt, no rightness or wrongness to a behavior pattern. These are spiritually dead individuals whom those in psychology call sociopaths. Anyone who claims lack of belief in the spiritual laws that govern morality are showing that they exist as the walking dead. This human being exists as if he is no different from a cat or dog in relation to behavior and belief systems.

I find it important to make this distinction because this is the basis for understanding who we are as human beings made in the image of our Creator. God exists in a physically non-tangible place in reality (the spirit).

We know and touch Him through behavior patterns and actions, for behavior is motivated by belief systems that are spiritual concepts. We do not experience Him in the physical (i.e., sight, hearing, touch, taste, smell). He is perfectly good because of how He always behaves in relation to others, not based on physical appearance. God is perfectly moral. Morality is not physical, but a behavioral construct.

> Will you steal and murder, commit adultery and perjury, burn incense to Baal and follow other gods you have not known, and then come and stand before me in this house, which bears my Name, and say, "We are safe"—safe to do all these detestable things? Has this house, which bears my Name, become a den of robbers to you? But I have been watching! declares the Lord.
>
> JEREMIAH 7:9—11

> Surely the arm of the Lord is not too short to save, nor his ear too dull to hear. But your iniquities have separated you from your God; your sins have hidden his face from you, so that he will not hear.
>
> ISAIAH 59:1—2

We all know individuals who claim that morality is a figment of the imagination. They say that what is right for you is fine and what is right for me is also fine, even if we are in conflict. They don't even consider the concept that someone could actually be right or wrong and, therefore, justified or not. They allow mutually exclusive concepts such as steal/not steal or cheat/not cheat or do/not do to exist in harmony, depending on the individual's personal belief at the time. This is the moral relativist. He exists alive as one of the walking dead.

This book speaks a message that he cannot and will not hear, for it is spiritually understood and he is dead to the spirit. You can only pray for such an individual, that God would free his mind from the lie (a spiritual law) that he has chosen to believe (a spiritual concept). Even as a dead man, he is moved by the laws of the spirit, although the polarity leads him toward death, not life (also spiritual and natural concepts).

The Fall of Man

All humans live somewhere along the spectrum of spiritual life and death depending on their understanding of the image of God that has been given to all persons. When our parents (Adam and Eve) ate of the tree, they experienced immediate spiritual death. Their eyes were open and they were able to see good and evil. Prior to this, they were only alive to God and the laws that led them toward life through obedience (a spiritual law). With the new understanding afforded them through rebellion (negative pole of obedience), they became alive to death and all the spiritual laws that led them in that direction.

This is what is meant when we speak of the fall of man. It is a fall from life toward death, obedience toward rebellion, light toward darkness, fidelity toward adultery, forgiveness toward shame, and good toward evil. It is a fall from the positive pole toward the negative pole of spirituality.

Satan used the spiritual law of disobedience (rebellion) to open their eyes to the polar universe that they existed in without their knowledge. And so it is now. We live in a polar universe, but with the knowledge of good and evil coupled with the capability of choice. We each must choose life or death with regard to the spiritual laws described above.

> This day I call heaven and earth as witnesses against you that I have set before you life and death, blessings and curses. Now choose life, so that you and your children may live and that you may love the Lord your God.
>
> Deuteronomy 30:19

These laws are the weapons wielded by the righteous. They are powerful in drawing us toward life, the polar extreme in which our Lord exists as completely alive. He is the God of all truth, forever faithful, full of forgiveness and goodness. God is perfectly alive spiritually.

The following is a list of scriptural examples that give support to my premise that God exists perfectly on the positive pole of spiritual behavior.

Forgiveness. "You are *forgiving* and good, O Lord, abounding in love to all who call to you" (Psalm 86:5, emphasis added).

Faith. "It is written: 'I believed; therefore I have spoken.' With that *same spirit of faith* we also believe and therefore speak" (2 Corinthians 4:13, emphasis added).

"Everything that does not come from *faith* is sin" (Romans 14:23, emphasis added).

"And without *faith* it is impossible to please God, because anyone who comes to him must believe that he exists and that he rewards those who earnestly seek him" (Hebrews 11:6, emphasis added).

Obedience. "Although he was a son, he learned *obedience* from what he suffered" (Hebrews 5:8, emphasis added).

Truth. "It is *impossible for God to lie*." (Hebrews 6:18, emphasis added).

"There are six things the Lord hates, seven that are detestable to him: haughty eyes, a lying tongue, hands that shed innocent blood, a heart that devises wicked schemes, feet that are quick to rush into evil, a false witness who pours out lies and a man who stirs up dissension among brothers" (Proverbs 6:16—19).

Fidelity. "Never will I leave you; never will I forsake you" (Hebrews 13:5).

"If we are faithless, he will remain *faithful*, for he cannot disown himself" (2 Timothy 2:13, emphasis added).

Sacrifice. "But now he has appeared once for all at the end of the ages to do away with sin by the *sacrifice* of himself" (Hebrews 9:26, emphasis added).

Humility. "Come to me, all you who are weary and burdened, and I will give you rest. Take my yoke upon you and learn from me, for I am gentle and *humble* in heart, and you will find rest for your souls. For my yoke is easy and my burden is light" (Matthew 11:28—30, emphasis added).

Hope. "We have this *hope* as an anchor for the soul, firm and secure" (Hebrews 6:19, emphasis added).

"Blessed is the man who trusts in the Lord, whose confidence is in him" (Jeremiah 17:7).

Good. "*I am the good* shepherd. The good shepherd lays down his life for the sheep" (John 10:11, emphasis added).

"Dear friend, do not imitate what is evil but what is *good*. Anyone who does what is *good* is from God. Anyone who does what is evil has not seen God" (3 John 1:11, emphasis added).

"To fear the Lord is to hate evil; I hate pride and arrogance, evil behavior and perverse speech" (Proverbs 8:13).

Pure/Holy/Clean. "Because it is written, be *holy*, because *I am holy*" (1 Peter 1:16, emphasis added).

"The Lord is righteous in all his ways, and *holy in all his works*" (Psalm 145:17 KJV, emphasis added).

"Dear friends, now we are children of God, and what we will be has not yet been made known. But we know that when he appears, we shall be like him, for we shall see him as he is. Everyone who has this hope in him purifies himself, just as he is *pure*" (1 John 3:2—3, emphasis added).

"For God did not call us to be im*pure*, but to live a *holy* life" (1 Thessalonians 4:7, emphasis added).

Marriage. "*Marriage* should be honored by all" (Hebrews 13:4, emphasis added).

"Turn, O backsliding children, saith the Lord; for *I am married* unto you" (Jeremiah 3:14 KJV, emphasis added).

"I hate divorce," says the Lord God of Israel" (Malachi 2:16).

Life. "In him was *life* and that life was the light of men" (John 1:4—5, emphasis added).

Light. "This is the message we have heard from him and declare to you: God is *light*; in him there is no darkness at all" (1 John 1:5, emphasis added).

Spiritually, our Lord is perfect and completely alive. "See, I set before you today life and prosperity (positive pole), death and destruction (negative pole).... Now choose life" (Deuteronomy 30:15, 19).

Jesus states, "Man does not live on bread alone (physical life), but on every word that comes from the mouth of God (spiritual life)" (Matthew 4:4). The first man and woman were deceived by Satan into breaking a spiritual law, not a natural one. With the breaking of a spiritual law, they moved toward spiritual death.

> And the Lord God commanded the man, "You are free to eat from any tree in the garden; but you must not eat from the tree of the knowledge of good and evil, for when you eat of it you will surely die."
>
> GENESIS 2:16—17

THE CONCEPT OF PARALLEL WORLDS

Man exists as natural and spiritual, and he is governed by the laws of both. Lack of belief in or understanding of this fact does not negate the reality of its existence. If an individual jumps from a building believing that he can fly, he will soon learn otherwise.

Scriptural backup for this can be seen as Jesus prays, "Our father in heaven, hallowed be your name, your kingdom come, your will be done on earth (physical) as it is in heaven (spiritual)" (Matthew 6:9—10).

> Beloved, I wish above all things that thou mayest prosper and be in health (physical), even as thy soul prospereth (spiritual).
>
> 3 JOHN 1:2 KJV

God created man to rule the earth (physical) as He ruled heaven (spiritual). In His image, He wanted us to rule, as He ruled.

> And let them rule over the fish of the sea and the birds of the air, over the livestock, over all the earth, and over all the creatures that move along the ground.
>
> GENESIS 1:26

We exist in a parallel universe (spiritual/physical). Our actions and behaviors connect us to our spiritual existence. We lean toward either life or death spiritually. As spiritual death takes hold, natural death soon follows, for spiritual death and physical death are intimately related.

I believe that aging and biological death are directly related to our spiritual life. Scripture states:

> By faith Enoch was taken from this life, so that he did not experience death; he could not be found, because God had taken him away. For before he was taken, he was commended as one who pleased God.
>
> HEBREWS 11:5

He told Moses that because of his disobedience he would not pass over into the Promised Land (Deuteronomy 32:48—52). He died without ever reaching it.

I also believe that spiritual sickness causes many forms of cancer and other physical ailments in humankind. In medicine, we see the concept of physical disease corresponding to sexual infidelity: sex that is not restricted to a covenant relationship. Physical transmission of disease to a sexual partner is in line with the spiritual concept of the one-flesh union described by God in Genesis. He states that "they will become one flesh" (Genesis 2:24). A sexual infidel will transmit physical disease even to a faithful partner. This is not a fault of the faithful, but a result of the unfaithful. Sexually transmitted diseases are manifested only in the sexually unclean (spiritual law).

Sex has a parallel purpose. It is a physical and spiritual union. Scripture states, "Do you not know that he who unites himself with a prostitute is one with her body? For it is said, The two will become one flesh. You were bought at a price. Therefore honor God with your body" (1 Corinthians 6:16, 20). Physical disease in one begets physical disease in another through sexual union, a natural and spiritual concept.

In medicine we see various forms of sickness that we term psychosomatic or mind-body illness. These would be physical manifestations of either pain or disease that is directly related to how an individual perceives the world around him. These are some of the most difficult patients to treat, mainly due to the fact that modern medicine is primarily focused on the physical and ignores the spiritual.

Physical medicine, at best, is only palliative for such individuals. The true healing will come only through spiritual insight into their belief systems and behavioral patterns. Personal insight, introspection, and humility are required to recognize flawed patterns of thinking in oneself. Most individuals possess too much pride to allow for the humility of introspection, a necessary ingredient for the spiritual healing that precedes physical healing. Modern medicine is focused on the physical aspects of illness. Spiritual counselors, pastors, guides, etc. focus on the spiritual. A marriage between the two offers the best chance for healing human sickness and disease.

Spiritual sickness can only be combated by spiritual wholeness. One or the other will win, for these will not exist together in a harmonious "one flesh" union. Scripture states:

> Do not be yoked together with unbelievers. For what do righteousness and wickedness have in common? Or what fellowship can light have with darkness?
>
> 2 CORINTHIANS 6:14

The Lord commanded Israel:

> Do not intermarry with them. Do not give your daughters to their sons or take their daughters for your sons, For they will turn your sons away from following me to serve other gods.
>
> DEUTERONOMY 7:3—4

Some individuals believe that this is scriptural evidence for not marrying outside of race. However, this is a flawed understanding of a spiritual commandment. Commandments are always given for our protection. All races of people are created in the image of God and, for this reason, are not physically unrelated.

God is not speaking to the physical differences of humankind in this account. He is speaking to the spiritual differences. You are either alive to God or dead to Him. It is unwise to join the living and the dead in a one-flesh union. Unbelief will defile belief, unclean will defile clean, and a lie will obscure the truth.

Sanctification is a concept of separation. God requires this of us for our own spiritual protection, not some foolish concept of racial superiority between human beings.

CHAPTER TWO

Sexual Sins

All forms of sexual sin violate some spiritual construct by which God restricts Himself in one form or another and is, therefore, not like God. All behaviors motivated by the negative pole of spirituality (e.g., selfishness, pride, rebellion, unforgiveness) are considered sin. The sexual union of man and animal is a physical and spiritual representation of opposites uniting as one. It is not allowed spiritually. This is the true meaning of racial superiority.

Sexual relations between men and animals are unthinkable. Animals are unrelated physically (genetically) and spiritually (they have none). We are so genetically and physically unrelated that chromosomal differences guarantee the fact that sexual contact with animals is incapable of producing life in the natural and is subsequently a physically dead act.

Spiritually, there is no union of existence with a vacuum (nothingness). It strikes to the core of what it means to have the oneness spoken of by God when He stated in regard to Adam and Eve, "The two will become one flesh." In the spirit, multiples equal one. Two become one in marriage and three are one in the Trinity (Father, Son, and Holy Spirit). Bestiality is one and nothingness, and therefore not one, but nothing. Bestiality is revealed by God as sin.

> Do not have sexual relations with an animal and defile yourself with it. A woman must not present herself to an animal to have sexual relations with it; that is a perversion.
>
> LEVITICUS 18:23

Pedophilia violates the spiritual law of sacrifice. In addition, the spiritual construct of covenant is ignored. God is a God of covenant (promise).

> Later I passed by, and when I looked at you and saw that you were old enough for love, I spread the corner of my garment over you and covered your nakedness. I gave you my solemn oath and entered into a covenant with you, declares the Sovereign Lord, and you became mine.
>
> EZEKIEL 16:8

In relation to His beloved, God promises to always be "xyz" as in a marriage one says his vows. Covenant can only be entered into by choice or consent. In the natural, the age of consent is debatable, but moving it down shows an agenda to prey on the physically and spiritually immature by way of their youth and lack of knowledge to protect themselves through conscientious choice.

Children have no sexual drive. The one who thinks otherwise is showing a predatory mind-set that believes a child has the right to sexual fulfillment. But what child is in need of sexual gratification? The pedophile looks to gain sexual satisfaction from the physically and spiritually immature. This is not an offering of sacrifice in which one suffers loss of something desirable to the self. Pedophiles, in self-absorption, take from others for themselves, regardless of the harm that may be involved. This violates the spiritual law of sacrifice and is the epitome of selfishness. Pedophilia is sin.

Polygamy violates the spiritual law of fidelity, the God-like behavior innate to feminine spirituality. Feminine fidelity is an important concept that I will expand on later in the text. God is faithful. He states:

Never will I leave you. Never will I forsake you.

HEBREWS 13:5

For this reason a man will leave his father and mother and be united to his wife, and they will become one flesh.

GENESIS 2:24

A deacon must be the husband of but one wife.

1 TIMOTHY 3:12

Each of these Scriptures implies the concept of spiritual fidelity. Polygamy dilutes the strength of masculinity and dishonors the feminine through loss of fidelity (a spiritual law).

It is important to understand the spiritual concepts of masculinity and femininity. They will be discussed in depth later. This understanding is imperative to the discussion of polygamist behavior. Polygamy violates the nature of spiritual masculinity and femininity. This will be covered further in chapter twelve, "An Equal Offering to Give."

Masturbation violates the spiritual law of sacrifice. It is inherently a selfish act engaged in only for the purpose of self-gratification. Physically, it is a dead act, for two do not become one. Furthermore, the male-female complement is lacking, which precludes creation of natural, physical life. Spiritually, it is dead because it offers nothing to another in the form of sacrifice. Selfishness is the death of sacrifice.

Then Judah said to Onan, "Lie with your brother's wife and fulfill your duty to her as a brother-in-law to produce offspring for your brother." But Onan knew that the offspring would not be his; so whenever he lay with his brother's wife, he spilled his semen on the ground to keep from producing offspring for his brother. What he did was wicked in the Lord's sight.

GENESIS 38:8—10

In this passage, we find the essence of masturbation, which is selfishness. Onan was self-absorbed. Obviously seeking sex in self-gratification, he cared nothing for the woman, who was the widow of his late brother. As was customary at that time, a man would lie with his dead brother's wife and bear children in his stead. This was intended for honor of his deceased brother. Onan's selfishness blocked fidelity to his brother and the widowed wife. Outside of sexual pleasure, he offered nothing.

Children bind two together as one in a living representation of a one-flesh union. They are a physical and spiritual sign of the one-flesh union. Selfishness is the opposite of sacrifice. Masturbation violates this spiritual law. This is a hard teaching for many, but nevertheless holds true to the spiritual laws of life and death.

Incest violates polarity. In nature, the positive and negative poles of a magnet will attract while similar poles repel. Sameness will repel in the spirit as well as the natural. Polarity/balance is a law by which all of creation functions, spiritually and physically. This is one reason homosexuality is considered sin. Brother and sister are opposites as male and female, but are the same with regard to a natural family construct. This form of the one-flesh union is not allowed spiritually.

> Do not have sexual relations with the daughter of your father's wife, born to your father; she is your sister.
>
> LEVITICUS 18:11

Leviticus chapter 18 discusses incest in its entirety. God commands us to abstain from all forms of it.

Fornication is sex outside the covenant of marriage. It violates every spiritual law (fidelity, sacrifice, obedience, covenant, etc.). Marriage is an institution whereby a male and a female promise to live as one, practicing through daily existence all of the spiritual laws that lead one toward God and life. As we will see in chapter six, "Sex, Marriage, and Obedience," the union of marriage contains every spiritual law. Therefore, all forms of sexual sin are considered fornication, as they all exist outside the confines of marriage.

Due to the social climate that surrounds the concept of homosexuality, this subject will be addressed in chapter eight, "Homosexuality and Gender Balance." It has been revealed by God as sin.

> Do not lie with a man as one lies with a woman; that is detestable.
>
> LEVITICUS 18:22

CHAPTER THREE

THE POWER OF LOVE

Man was made to have dominion on earth (Genesis 1:26) as God has dominion in heaven. Heaven is God's throne and earth is His footstool (Matthew 5:34—35). We are made in the image of God to rule earth as He rules heaven in love, the greatest of all. "And now these three remain: faith, hope and love. But the greatest of these is love" (1 Corinthians 13:13).

Marriage is a love covenant (promise) between a man and woman who choose to share their lives together. This union contains all aspects of the positive pole governing spiritual behaviors (e.g., forgiveness, faith, hope, sacrifice, humility, fidelity). Behavior consistent with the positive pole is called love behavior and it carries spiritual power.

Love is a choice, not a feeling. Feelings may change for different reasons, usually based on new experiences in reference to one's surroundings. Love is a decision consistent with the positive pole of spirituality. It will change only as an act of the will. Marriage, simply put, is a promise to love. This is undoubtedly the character that drives our Lord's behavior with regard to us in relationship to Him. He wants us to rule earth with the same character by which He rules. We are made in the image of God in every way, and we are made to reflect His character on earth. God's character is love.

In the beginning God gave man authority over the earth (Genesis 1:28). The basis of that dominion would be mediated through what Adam knew and what was modeled to him by God. God knew that He needed to model dominion for the man in order for him to understand what it meant for the earth to obey him.

This was the reason behind the tree of the knowledge of good and evil. God commanded Adam not to eat from it. In the absence of sin (fear, rebellion, selfishness, doubt, shame, negative pole of spirituality, etc.) faith was pure. That was the basis for Adam's belief in the instructions given to him by God. Scripture states, "But without faith it is impossible to please him" (Hebrews 11:6 KJV). This pure, childlike faith in the authority given to him by God gave power to the commandment of Adam in the earth. After the fall, Adam's faith was no longer pure. It became tainted by fear, the polar opposite of faith. Fear is not of God.

> There is no fear in love. But perfect love drives out fear.... The one who fears is not made perfect in love.
>
> 1 JOHN 4:18

Faith is a component of love, and it carries spiritual power. It is understandable that perfect love would cast out fear, as faith is the polar opposite of fear and they cannot dwell together in harmony.

After Adam and Eve ate of the tree that God had commanded them not to eat, they immediately experienced fear.

> But the Lord God called to the man, "Where are you?" He answered, "I heard you in the garden, and I was afraid because I was naked; so I hid." And he said, "Who told you that you were naked? Have you eaten from the tree that I commanded you not to eat from?"
>
> GENESIS 3:9—11

He hid because he was afraid. Why was he afraid? Fear is not of God. Faith, the opposite of fear, is rooted in love, which is God. Where did his fear come from? He had not experienced it before. It came from the separation from God's presence through disobedience.

Disobedience/rebellion is sin. It is connected to the negative polarities of spiritual behaviors (e.g., rebellion, unbelief, fear, shame/guilt, selfishness, adultery, lies, evil, death, etc.). As one positive spiritual behavior attract others, one negative spiritual behavior attract other negatives. Disobedience opened the door to fear through this polar communion of spiritual laws.

Even today, all forms of disobedience/rebellion, whether in regard to parent-child relationships or legal, societal law, bring the fear of justice for violation of law. This is the effect of what it means to know good and evil. Adam no more knew what faith was than he did fear or rebellion prior to the fall. He lived in faith and all other aspects of love without even knowing it, for God had only modeled to him what existed in Himself. He modeled goodness.

The experience of one form of sin behavior (rebellion) opened the door to its counterparts as well. Adam now understood rebellion by experience. He also learned of fear, which is intimately related. Shame was sure to follow as Adam noticed his nakedness. Nakedness is a sign of vulnerability and exposure.

Prior to the fall, Scripture states, "They were both naked, the man and his wife, and were not ashamed" (Genesis 2:25 KJV). They were not ashamed because their nakedness was only connected to what God had given them. He had given them only goodness. Even their bodies were good. The connection of shame to nakedness came from the exposure they felt through violation of the commandment of God. God asked, "Who told you that you were naked? Have you eaten from the tree that I commanded you not to eat from?" (Genesis 3:11). How else would he have learned fear? Fear would never have existed in Adam had he not learned disobedience. How else would he have learned shame? Shame would not have existed had he not learned fear.

Adam and Eve were deceived into disobedience. They had no ability in themselves to disobey. Nowhere in their existence was disobedience modeled for them. Satan knew that in order to get God's children to fall, he had to deceive them into it. So he lied to the man and woman. This was the first lie ever told. That is why Scripture tells us that Satan is the father of lies

(John 8:44). He was a liar from the beginning (John 8:44). Subsequently, lying is one of the great abominations that God hates.

> There are six things the Lord hates, seven that are detestable to him: haughty eyes, a lying tongue, hands that shed innocent blood, a heart that devises wicked schemes, feet that are quick to rush into evil, a false witness who pours out lies and a man who stirs up dissension among brothers. ... And all liars—their place will be in the fiery lake of burning sulfur.
>
> Proverbs 6:16—19; Revelation 21:8

A lie caused God's creation, man, to fall away from Him. The man and woman had no concept of a lie. When Satan told it, they believed it. They then learned disobedience by their actions, contrasted by the light of God's commandment that they should not eat.

With his faith no longer pure and the added problems of fear, shame, etc., Adam no longer looked like God in reference to his feelings or behavioral patterns. In that instant, Adam and Eve died spiritually. God's image had been tainted by sin, and the authority and power that went along with the image began to fade. Their bodies also began the natural process of decay that precedes physical death.

God never intended for Adam and Eve to die physically. That was a choice they made through disobedience, which connected them to death (first spiritually and then physically).

> And the Lord God said, "The man has now become like one of us, knowing good and evil. He must not be allowed to reach out his hand and take also from the tree of life and eat, and live forever." So the Lord God banished him from the Garden of Eden to work the ground from which he had been taken. After he drove the man out, he placed on the east side of the Garden of Eden cherubim and a flaming sword flashing back and forth to guard the way to the tree of life.
>
> Genesis 3:22—24

It would be interesting indeed to have experienced the life of Adam and Eve prior to their fall from power. But Scripture gives us insight into what it means to have dominion over the earth. The Bible speaks of a second Adam, Jesus. He presented Himself as God in the flesh to destroy the works of Satan and restore, by example and sacrifice (spiritual law), what it means to be man, bearing the image of our creator. Jesus walked the earth as Adam walked prior to the fall.

What does that walk look like? It starts with perfect, God-like behavior (faith, humility, sacrifice, belief, fidelity, forgiveness, goodness, and all the other things Jesus is known for). It also looks like the original authority over the earth that was initially given to Adam by God (Genesis 1:28). Jesus commanded the seas, "Peace, be still" (Mark 4:39 KJV). The disciples asked, "What manner of man is this, that even the winds and the sea obey him!" (Matthew 8:27 KJV).

Devils recognize when a man understands and believes in his God-given authority. The man afflicted with many demons ran up to Jesus, saying, "Ha! What do you want with us, Jesus of Nazareth? Have you come to destroy us? I know who you are—the Holy One of God!"

"Be quiet!" Jesus said sternly. "Come out of him!" (Luke 4:34—35).

Based on the perfect, God-like behavior modeled by Jesus Christ, He was able to accomplish the miracles that were given to man in the beginning when God gave Adam authority over the earth. With the experience of sin, Adam lost his power. It is not that man no longer had authority. Rather, man no longer was perfect in love (containing all spiritual laws on the positive pole of spirituality), which is the requirement for wielding God-like power.

The disciples asked Jesus why they could not cast out the demon. Jesus said their failure was due to their unbelief (Matthew 17:19–20). Unbelief is driven by fear. Fear is contrary to faith, which is a requirement for God's authority and power to work. Scripture states that with faith the size of a mustard seed we could speak to a mountain and command it to be cast into the sea and it would obey us.

> I tell you the truth, if you have faith as small as a mustard seed, you can say to this mountain, "Move from here to there" and it will move. Nothing will be impossible for you.
>
> MATTHEW 17:20

Jesus is explaining to us how things ought to be based on how God set them up in the beginning. He was our example of how we were meant to walk on this earth. This is the authority that He spoke of: the authority to command the seas, the winds, the earth, demons, etc. He showed us that it is possible. Jesus said that we would do even greater miracles than He (John 14:12).

Scripture speaks of the earth groaning for the authority of the sons of God (Romans 8:19, 22). I believe the earth is out of balance. We see this in natural disasters such as typhoons, hurricanes, tornadoes, earthquakes, etc. The earth is, for certain, groaning and in pain. Jesus calmed the seas, spoke to the winds, and fed five thousand people with five loaves of bread and two fish (John 6). It appears that He was bringing peace and calm to an earth set off balance by the fall of man.

We must all seek to become more and more transformed into the image of God, through love and its components, in order to live as we were created to exist on the earth. When your actions are motivated by love, this authority and power will exist for you. Love is the basis of the authority and power we have. God rules heaven with benevolence and love. We are in His image and are required to do the same. If you don't, you have no legitimate power. It is not that your authority over the earth does not exist, "for God's gifts and his call are irrevocable" (Romans 11:29). But God will not give His authority to those who do not display His character. Without love, one would use this power and authority toward selfish (negative pole) ends.

It is common practice for Christians to try to use this concept of faith for personal and selfish gain. We hear of individuals using faith to try to receive wealth without first sacrificing (positive pole) their attitudes and lives to God. This is, basically, the worship of money. They believe for selfish gain. They pray for wealth and prosperity while being delinquent on debts already owed. They have not learned temperance and have not dealt faithfully with what has already been given to them. They have not known God to the extent of His desired involvement in their personal affairs. They are fooling themselves if they believe they will receive their request of financial overflow from God if they are not alive to him in what little they have already been given.

God is not against the prosperity of His people. But He cannot be fooled into blessing someone with wealth when He knows that individual cannot be trusted to deal justly with it. "For the love of money is a root of all kinds of evil" (1 Timothy 6:10).

Jesus states the greatest commandment:

> Love the Lord your God with all your heart and with all your soul and with all your mind. This is the first and greatest commandment. And the second is like it: love your neighbor as yourself. All the Law and the Prophets hang on these two commandments.
>
> MATTHEW 22:37—40

He will not risk you creating an idol out of money if you have not learned to sacrifice all for Him. This includes attitudes and behaviors. Individuals who do not routinely give to the less fortunate will not be entrusted with more.

Furthermore, a wife who lives in defiance and disobedience to a husband is fooling herself when she prays in faith to receive the blessings of God. Scripture states, "When you ask, you do not receive, because you ask with wrong motives, that you may spend what you get on your pleasures" (James 4:3). Anything that is not love is sin.

By requiring love of His image bearers, God assures that strength and power will only exist under the narrow auspices of fidelity to love. God has decreed man's dominion over the earth. This is the way it is. When we speak in faith, believing, these things can and will be done. However, we can only be held to the standards by which God holds Himself. If you are not experiencing the power of God in your life, a careful examination is in order. You may be surprised at what you find.

CHAPTER FOUR

HUMAN DEVELOPMENT
(SPIRITUAL AND PHYSICAL)

MODELED BEHAVIOR (SPIRITUAL)

God is a God of order. Obedience is required for order. God is in charge of heaven. Man is in charge of earth (Genesis). God had to require obedience from man in order to model dominion to him. How could man rule without having God model it for him? The commandment had to come to show the man obedience.

Only by learning obedience to God could man require obedience from the earth. Man's rule would be accomplished through what Adam knew based on what God had shown him through modeled behavior. Without this modeling of dominion by God, Adam would not have understood obedience, or rebellion for that matter. How could Adam rule without a concept of these polar spiritual laws?

As it was in the beginning, so it continues to be now. Our children are replicas of what Adam was to God in the beginning. Though in the form of an adult man, Adam was actually a child spiritually. With childhood comes innocence. He would only understand his environment based on what was given to him through instruction and a type of modeled behavior.

Children learn best not by the giving of instruction, but a modeling of the desired behavior. This instruction, coupled with modeling, assures the child's understanding of what the behavior means by practical application. Parents who continually chastise a child for a particular undesirable behavior should not be surprised to find that behavior a common problem in their own lives. Where else will a child (a blank slate from the beginning) learn yelling, hitting, or other forms of socially unacceptable behavior if not from his primary models of what it means to exist in the world? These models are the parents or other individuals responsible for the primary nurturing of the children.

This is why it is so important for parents (male and female), made in God's image, to display God's nature (love). This guarantees children who will do and be the same. Children do not comprehend the idea of God, but they will see His character and image in their parents. When the age of reasoning arrives, they will understand who He is by comparing Him to what they have seen and experienced in the parents. If they have experienced love, they will believe that there is a supreme lover, God. If they do not experience love, they may have difficulty understanding the concept of love. Hence, they will have difficulty comprehending God, for "God is love" (1 John 4:8 KJV).

The atheist's mind is devoid of the concept of love. He believes that God is not present with us. He claims to have no belief in a supreme being that says, "Never will I leave you; never will I forsake you" (Hebrews 13:5). This is the concept of fidelity, a component of love. Undoubtedly, one can always find difficulties in regard to his parent-child relationships. This is often the source of a major emotional wound, either consciously understood or unconsciously experienced through denial (covered in depth in chapter fifteen, "The Healing of Man").

Love contains all elements of self-sacrifice. This includes time spent with children, providing for them financially, protecting them from harm emotionally and physically, providing instruction, even discipline. Scripture states, "Endure hardship as discipline; God is treating you as sons. For what son is not disciplined by his father? If you are not disciplined (and everyone undergoes discipline), then you are illegitimate children and not true sons" (Hebrews 12:7—8). If these elements are not in the parent-child relationship, the parent is not showing love for the child.

You do not love a child whom you will not provide for. You do not love a child whom you do not spend time with. You do not love a child whom you will not discipline. You do not love a child whom you will not protect. Children bear the image of God. They feel the same thing God feels when we show lack of love for Him: pain.

> The Lord saw how great man's wickedness on the earth had become, and that every inclination of the thoughts of his heart was only evil all the time. The Lord was grieved that he had made man on the earth, and his heart was filled with pain.
>
> GENESIS 6:5—6

If you fail to display patterns of love behavior to your children, they will feel as if you do not love them. They will have internal pain. If they don't believe that you love them, you will not receive love in return. God sets the example. He models love to us in order to show us how to love in return. "We love him, because he first loved us" (1 John 4:19 KJV). Disobedient, rebellious children are showing the signs of an emotional wound inflicted in some way by the parent toward whom their rebellion is directed. My pastor preached on this subject once. He put it this way, in reference to the parent-child relationship: "What they see is what you get."

Children have to learn by teaching. We are God's children, and we must learn by being taught and having rules established. God is the giver of all rules. He is our Father. We are to worship and serve Him only. Satan tempted Jesus to bow down and worship him. Jesus replied, "Away from me, Satan! For it is written: Worship the Lord your God, and serve him only" (Matthew 4:10). As in the natural, children also learn spiritually by modeling. They will learn of God by seeing both parents expressing love in their relationship. Without relationship one to another (polarity), love does not exist.

Love embodies all of the spiritual polarities that are rooted in God-like behavior. Hence love, behavior, and relationship take their appropriate places in connection with the realm of morality rooted in God. As children grow and learn of their own imperfections, this will allow room for their parents' imperfections and facilitate forgiveness. As they see our failures to model His image perfectly, they will begin to understand that we are only trying to model God's image. He *is* the image.

THE PHYSIOLOGY OF BEHAVIOR (PHYSICAL)
NEUROPLASTICITY AND ADDICTION

A child from birth to three years of age is a wonder to behold. Babies come into this world completely innocent, understanding nothing about the world they have just become a part of. They have no willful or conscientious actions. Even feeding is mediated by primitive reflexes void of willful acting capability. These reflexes are generated in the lower areas of the brain (spinal cord and brainstem) responsible for innate behaviors (e.g., routing, sucking, palmar-grasp reflexes).These reflexes are seen universally in newborns, as the higher brain, the neocortex, has not yet been trained to suppress such activities through conscious activity and trained behaviors.

The neocortex is the large, dome-like section of the brain responsible for willful action, thought, reasoning, and communication. In infants this portion of the brain has plasticity, amenable to development and change, capable of learning, malleable. It is underdeveloped but has more capability at birth than at any other time in the individual's existence.

At this stage in development the brain begins to learn about itself and the surroundings into which the individual has been born. This learning takes place by means of complicated neuronal connections that are established hourly as the child experiences the environment around him. In essence, the physical structure of the brain is modified daily by experience and subsequent actions performed by the individual in this stage of development. The brain at birth is a blank slate. The child will become what he sees, experiences, and does based on his environmental stimuli.

As the child matures, the brain enlarges. This larger, more specific brain (neocortex) has generated capabilities compatible with adults in regard to active, willful activity connected with personal choice. As maturity continues, this plastic phase of brain growth and development diminishes greatly. Furthermore, as one ages, we see the natural loss of neocortical brain tissue, leading to the expected return of infantile reflexes and loss of higher brain functions associated with age-related dementia (Alzheimer's disease).

Language, one of the most complicated and fascinating facets of human existence, is developed in the first three years of life. After this, different languages will never be grasped as quickly and easily as they were during this highly neuro-plastic phase of human brain development. Regardless of race, the child will speak with the accent of the culture in which he is reared from infancy. Language and dialect are functions of culture, not biology.

Infantile neuro-plastic development is also the time when children learn about gender, another concrete reality to the existence of humanity. By the age of two years, many children can distinguish between male, female, and socially acceptable behavior patterns of each. This includes the understanding of their own connection to the gender in which they belong. As Adam was to God a plastic child, so are our children in relation to what they see, hear, and experience, primarily from an individual considered responsible for the child's growth and development. This is a major factor in the environment of any infant child and likely the primary mechanism by which the child obtains values, beliefs, and ideas regarding social interaction with the environment at large.

Though such plasticity diminishes during maturity, the adult brain continues to possess the capabilities of change, learning, and growth, though not to the degree of the infant brain. We see evidence of this in the science surrounding habits, compulsions, and subsequent addiction.

Opium is a substance derived from the opium poppy, a seed plant found in nature. It is the base ingredient in the medical narcotic called morphine, a pain killer. It is processed chemically to produce the street drug heroin. The pleasure, excitement, and pain-blocking responses are mediated by natural opioid (opium-like) chemicals called neurotransmitters, a type of central nervous system hormone. These substances are released during times of stress, pain, and the intense pleasure associated with sexual activity and orgasm. If continuously exposed to high levels of these hormones, the brain becomes refractory; it loses its capability to respond normally (down regulation). This produces a biochemical situation in which more hormones are needed to produce the same level of response generated during earlier times of exposure.

In the case of heroin addiction, continued external (outside) supply causes the body to decrease its own endogenous (inside/internal) production of hormones. Once the body has lost its capability to produce a normal supply of hormones, if a continued external supply is not furnished, we eventually see a relative lack of body opioid supply. This produces the phenomenon commonly known as heroin (or narcotic) withdrawal. It is associated with a subjective experience of extreme physical pain, stress, anxiety, and a fiend-like search for the relief that comes with introduction of more heroin into the body system.

This suppression of endogenous opium is a progressive process. Repeated exposure causes the down regulation. At first, heroin users are free to choose. But as time passes, the brain develops synaptic connections (the way one nerve connects to another in order to stimulate a particular action) that support a particular behavior choice. This is a result of the residual neuro-plasticity associated with the adult brain. As the brain becomes wired to a particular behavior pattern, the compounding effect of opioid withdrawal produces a profound, almost uncontrollable drive to return to a particular behavioral choice. The behavior comes with an expected pleasure response and subsequent relief of internal pain.

This is the physiology of addition. It starts out as a willful choice, but when compounded by the expected rearrangement of brain structure (plasticity) and deranged neurochemical physiology (down regulation), it becomes a compulsion/addiction behavior. These individuals experience a near complete loss of willful capability to resist a particular behavior. The behavior is driven by an organically diseased physiologic state.

In addiction physiology, we see a condition that is ultimately the effect of initial willful choice compounded by a physical drive that supports it. These individuals are also prone to extreme bouts of depression during periods of opioid lack due to the nature of these substances to act as natural mood enhancers.

Sexual addiction is mediated by the same physiology. The difference lies in the fact that sexual excitement and orgasm are a result of behavioral activity, not external chemical supplementation. Initially, a typical behavior drives the expected sexual orgasmic response. This could be any behavior associated with the ability to achieve orgasm. Examples include sexual intercourse, pornography coupled with masturbation, voyeurism, phone sex, or even olfactory-derived nosmias (smell responses). Regardless of the type of activity, the progression to orgasm produces the pleasure response.

The above describes a symbiotic relationship between choice and physiology. Initial choices, if allowed to persist, will ultimately result in physical changes in the brain. These changes make future choices more likely to mimic the former by two pathways, plasticity and neurochemical dysregulation.

> The cortex is arranged in large clusters of densely interconnected neurons. Each cell establishes connections, sometimes at great distances, to as many as a hundred thousand other cells. It is also the part of the brain whose connections between neurons will be slowly modified over time, strengthening some connections, weakening others, and eliminating some entirely—all based on how experience shapes us. This ongoing process embeds the emerging pattern of our choices ever more firmly in actual tissue changes. ... Behaviors become increasingly strengthened through repetition. This strengthening physically alters the brain in a way that cannot be entirely undone, if at all; it is modified with great difficulty. Such modification requires a greater effort of will, additional repetition of the new behavior, and more time the more deeply embedded in the brain the old behavior has become.[3]

This concept keeps step with my initial premise of parallel worlds. Where choice and behavior represent the spiritual, plasticity and neurochemical physiology represent the natural. In the end, spiritual choices affect the physical aspects of our existence. Our particular sins become written on the tablets of our physical beings. This is ultimate self-determination. After all has been said, we choose our current realities one decision at a time.

The following Jewish/Christian fable is a perfect illustration of this concept of behavioral addiction. I define it as "addiction physiology initially supported by our willful choices." I will quote it in its entirety, along with the author's comments as a post-thought.

> One day long ago, over the hot sands of a middle-Eastern country, a white skylark flew in joyous loops about the sky. As she swooped near the earth, she heard a merchant cry out, "Worms! Worms! Worms for feathers! Delicious worms!"
>
> The skylark circled about the merchant, hungry at the mention of worms, but puzzled as to what the merchant meant. Little did the skylark know that the merchant was the devil. And seeing that the skylark was interested, the devil motioned her nearer. "Come here, my little friend. Come! See the lovely worms I have!"
>
> Cautiously, the skylark landed and cocked her head at the merchant. "Come! Taste the juicy worms!" The skylark became aware that she was, indeed, quite hungry. And these worms looked bigger and tastier than any she had ever dug for herself out of the hardscrabble ground of the desert. The skylark hopped closer and put her beak up close to the worm. "Two worms for a feather, my friend. Two worms for one!"
>
> The skylark was unable to resist. And she had, after all, so many feathers. So, with a swift motion, she pulled out a feather—just a small one—from beneath her wing and gave it to the merchant. "Take your pick, my little friend…any two, your heart's desire!" And so the skylark quickly snatched up two of the plumpest worms and swallowed her meal with delight. Never before had she tasted such wonderful worms. With a loud chirp, she leapt into the air and resumed her joyful flight.
>
> Day after day the skylark returned. And always the merchant had wonderful worms to offer: black ones and blue ones, red ones and green ones, all fat and shiny and iridescent. But one day, after eating her fill, the skylark leapt again into the air—and to her horror, she fell to the ground with a thud. She was unable to fly!
>
> All at once, with a shock, she realized what had happened. From the delicious worms she had grown fatter and fatter; and as

she plucked her feathers one by one, first her body, then her tail, and finally her very wings had grown balder and balder. Horrified, she remembered how, slowly, imperceptibly, day by day, it had been getting harder and harder to fly; and how she had told herself it was no matter; she could always stop before it was too late. Now, suddenly, here she was, trapped on the ground. She looked up and saw the merchant looking at her. Was that a small, sly grin spreading across his face?

In terror, the skylark ran off into the desert. She ran and ran and ran and ran. It took her hours and hours. Never in her entire life had she walked nor run so far. Finally, she came to the softer ground near the desert springs where, before she met the merchant, she daily had come to dig for herself the small, dusty brown desert worms that could be found around the springs.

The skylark dug and dug in a frenzy. She piled up worm after worm until it was nearly dark. Then, wrapping her catch in a small fallen palm frond, she dragged it off back across the sand to where she saw the merchant, closing up his stall for the night.

The skin around her beak had grown bruised and tender; her small feet were bleeding from the great distances she had been forced to walk. "Oh, merchant! Oh, merchant! Please help me! Please help me! I cannot fly anymore! Oh, dear what shall I do? Please, please, take these worms from me and give me back my feathers!"

The merchant bent down and peered at the terrified skylark. He threw back his head and roared with laughter, a gold tooth glinting in the red and setting sunlight. "Oh, I'll take those worms all right, my friend. A few weeks in this good soil and they too, will be fat and green and glistening." He un-wrapped the worms and tossed them into a jar of black and humid soil. "But feathers?" He laughed again. "What will you do with feathers? Glue them on with spit?" He wheezed and cackled at his little joke.

"Besides, my friend," the merchant reached down and grabbed the already plucked and fattened skylark, "that's not my business—'feathers for worms.' Oh no." He threw the skylark into a cage. "My business is 'WORMS FOR FEATHERS!'" The merchant slammed the little cage door shut, smiled hungrily at his victim, and with a loud SNAP! Of his fingers, he vanished into the desert air.

As our fable tells us, each time we behave in a certain way—each time the skylark exchanges a feather for worms—there is an important sense in which we choose to do so. And each time we do, we tell ourselves the truth that we are free to choose not to. Yet it is also true that with each successive step we progressively lose the ability to turn around, and yet are unaware of this worsening, insidious moral incapacitation. This is the devil's bargain we make with each successive step we take. At the end, it seems we are completely trapped, and can no more undo the changes in ourselves we have thereby allowed to develop—indeed, changes in the very brain—than can the leopard change his spots or the skylark buy back her feathers. From this trap there may eventually become no escape—none, that is, without the help of God.[4]

It is a well-documented phenomenon that sex addiction and other compulsive forms of sexual deviancy are fraught with the same problems of social dysfunction and isolation as chemical addicts. Addiction draws a person toward an internal spiral of self-preoccupation, search of pleasure, and release. The compulsive behaviors take precedence over familial relationships and friendships. For the sexual or chemical addict, there will always be difficulties with interpersonal relating. This extreme self-preoccupation precludes intimacy, especially in a spousal environment. Spouses bear the burden associated with the ineffectual relating capabilities of chemical and sexual addicts. Typical complaints center around a perceived distance or withdrawn emotional unavailability.

---

[3]Jeffrey Satinover, MD, *Homosexuality and the Politics of Truth* (Grand Rapids, MI: Hamewith Books, and imprint of Baker Book House, 1996), 135—136, 139.
[4]Jeffrey Satinover, MD, *Homosexuality and the Politics of Truth* (Grand Rapids, MI: Hamewith Books, and imprint of Baker Book House, 1996), 130—133.

Chapter Five

Behold the Image

Gender

Man possesses a likeness to God in the fact that we are governed by all the polar, spiritual laws that move the spirit realm in relation to morality. This is only a portion of His image that we bear. We also look like God in the way that we feel and behave in relation to stimuli. This is what I call gender.

Gender is a polarity of behavior and response patterns that governs the spiritual universe. Unlike the polar spiritual laws spoken of up to this point (e.g., faith, forgiveness, humility, obedience), it is not a moral construct. It can best be described as action and response patterns or gender response.

God states, "Let us make man in our image, after our likeness…male and female created he them" (Genesis 1:26, 27 KJV). When God created man, gender was a basis for which we were to bear his likeness. This does not mean that God is male or female, as I will elaborate on shortly.

God has a set of behavior and response patterns that sometimes appear to contradict one another. However, in any situation, the gender behavior is neither a right nor a wrong response, and carries no moral value. Gender has nothing to do with morality.

Let's say a child disobeys a rule established in the home. The father immediately moves toward corrective action while the mother strives to cover the child in mercy. In this example the father is behaving out of a masculine gender pattern described as justice, while the mother responds out of the feminine gender pattern described as mercy. It is neither right nor wrong to show a child justice. Nor is it either right or wrong to show a child mercy.

Here's another example of gender responsiveness. A family of three—father, mother, and child—are spending an afternoon at the park. Out of nowhere, a large dog appears and makes his way toward the child. The mother instinctively runs to the child to offer feminine comfort while the father instinctively moves toward the dog in an offering of masculine self-sacrifice and protection. It is neither right nor wrong to offer comfort or protection. Both would be needed in this scenario.

Gender action/response patterns are the yin and yang of behavior. Gender is a spiritual law by which all of creation functions. Man and woman are the natural side of the parallel universe with regard to gender. They are not a concept, but a physical reality that we can see, touch, hear, and smell. Masculine and feminine behavior patterns are associated with the spiritual side of the parallel universe. Masculinity acts while femininity responds/receives. It is neither right nor wrong to act or respond. In all cases, both are required.

Masculinity and femininity are not physical realities. They are spiritual concepts governing behavior patterns. Men may possess masculine or feminine behavior patterns. Women may possess masculine or feminine behavior patterns. As feminine we receive and as masculine we give or pass on. In the natural realm, it is the man who determines the genetic gender of his offspring. This is a scientific fact. Woman will bring forth only what she has been given.

Male and *female* are terms that take into account the duality of natural gender (man/woman) and spiritual gender (masculinity/femininity). Woman is the primary bearer of the feminine image of God (spiritual responsiveness) and man is the primary bearer of the masculine image of God (spiritual giving).

When we think of male and female, we see a physical makeup with a corresponding behavior pattern. Men are expected to be masculine and women are expected to be feminine. God called them male and female. This takes into account the duality of their existence as natural and spiritual beings. When a baby is born male, you should expect that child to look a certain way (manly) and act a certain way (masculine). The same is expected with a female baby.

Norms of masculine and feminine concepts are universally accepted across different societies. However, there are also cultural aspects to what we consider masculine and feminine behavior. For example, a kilt is a traditional knee-length pleated skirt worn by men in certain areas of northern Scotland. In American culture, it would be unthinkable for men to wear skirts. Now, skirts, in themselves, have no inherent masculine or feminine qualities. The culture assigns a gender value to them. An individual will find it necessary to conform his gender behavior and attire according to the culture of which he is a part. Otherwise, he will find himself out of step with his social environment. This brings all the difficulties of social relating that plague many subcultures in any society.

It is imperative to make the distinction here between God and man. God is neither a man nor a woman. He is neither male nor female. God is spirit. He possesses no physical attributes of men or women. In the sense of cultural gender norms, God has no image. I do not believe in the concept of a physical representation of God. Physical images of God bring Him into this world instead of understanding His true nature, which is spiritual, not natural/physical. He has a spiritual gender image, not a physical one.

Because God is spirit, He has behavioral patterns that are reflected in man. Some of those behavioral patterns are more clearly expressed in men and some in women. This is the balance of God in the earth. The terms *male* and *female* describe a physical nature that corresponds to a spiritual behavior pattern. God does not have a dual nature. This duality is only true of humankind.

Man and woman are physical terms alone. It does not guarantee any particular behavioral pattern. Masculine and feminine are behavioral attributes. They do not necessarily correspond to any physical makeup. When we speak of God as masculine and feminine, we do not speak of a physical idea. Ascribing the terms *man* or *woman* to God is not appropriate. God has behavioral attributes, and behavior is spiritual. The ones that are more clearly seen in women (e.g., forgiveness, mercy, submission, beauty, receiving, nurturing, fidelity, comforting, following, relating, intuition, being, encompassing, bringing forth life) are viewed as feminine qualities. The ones that are more clearly expressed in men (e.g., leading, governing, ruling, protecting, providing, giving, executing justice, doing, acting, exploring, being duty based, focused, straight to the point, law based, practical, using verifiable knowledge) are viewed as masculine qualities of God.

These masculine and feminine qualities are not universally bestowed upon any man or woman. Gender behavior is fluid. Men can possess feminine qualities and women can possess masculine ones. But the primary gender behavior of any human will be in line with the physical gender status given by God.

Spiritually, men are more masculine than they are feminine and women are more feminine than they are masculine. Instead of calling these behavioral patterns *masculine* and *feminine*, we could define them as "Y" patterns or "X" patterns. However, that would obscure the concept of what it means to be made in God's image as male and female. Furthermore, it would play into the fears of the prevailing modern belief that men and women are the same and that we should not embrace our unique gender roles.

Scripturally, male and female are both parts of God's image. However, God is not male or female. Human beings have both a physical and a spiritual nature. God is spirit. To be made in His image means that we possess a spiritual nature analogous to that of God. Man's physical nature is ours alone.

The fact that we possess physical gender may cloud the fact that the spiritual/behavioral counterpart is only the parallel side of the coin (parallel world). The difficulties we have with the gender balance of God is a reflection of our focus on the physical nature of gender. Ascribing to God man/woman (physical) or male/female (physical combined with spiritual) qualities puts Him in our image, not vice versa.

God has behavioral patterns that give balance to the earth. Men and women are relational beings created in His image. God is love, which is a behavior specific to the polarities of life. This can be a difficult concept to grasp. But when we learn to see God the way He truly is, we will realize that we are merely fallen replicas (image bearers) of the perfect.

The Qualities of Gender

God has a perfect balance of both masculine and feminine qualities. His masculine justice is balanced equally by His feminine mercy. His masculinity gives us a Savior in Christ, and His femininity allows Him to receive us as children. As a masculine father, He disciplines us as children (Hebrews 12:6—7), and as a feminine mother, He comforts us in our pain. "Praise be to the God and Father of our Lord Jesus Christ, the Father of compassion and the God of all comfort, who comforts us in all our troubles" (2 Corinthians 1:3—4). His image is balanced. He is not a God of justice only-that would have left us without a Savior. He is not a God of mercy only-that would negate our need for Jesus.

God said, "Let us make man in our image, after our likeness.... So God created man in his own image, in the image of God created he him; male and female created he them" (Genesis 1:26—27 KJV). God named man "man." He named woman "woman." He gave the concepts of masculine and feminine that correspond to the man and woman created in His image. He wanted His creation to reflect the balance that exists in Himself. Gender is how God reflects His spiritual balance here on earth. We are made in His image, for we bear His spiritual likeness in our existence as male and female.

Different spiritual qualities come with each gender. Everyone knows there is an inherent difference between men and women. We think differently, learn differently, and are generally motivated by different ideas. These differences are spiritual, and they are based on the gender identity given to us by God. This is immutable, regardless of the lie being proclaimed in the world today that claims equality based on similarity. Viewing men and women as similar with regard to roles and purpose obscures the lines between genders and subsequently blurs our vision of God.

Man can be easily motivated by such things as wealth, power, strength, status, achievement, and conquering. He is more analytical and objective in his thinking than woman and less likely to act based on emotion. He is active in doing and competition (sports) and likely to have many friendships based on shared interests or activities. He is mechanical, a worker, and prone to find significance and worth in his work. He desires respect. He is playful and adventurous, prone to exploration of his environment. He wants to know why something works the way it does. These are the "boys and their toys."

Woman is primarily a creature of feeling. She is receptive. Her emotions run deep. She is expressive and likely to be motivated by desire for intimacy and closeness in relationships rather than financial prosperity or conquest. Friendships are generally limited to a few trusted companions. Her primary desire is toward relationship and closeness with her spouse. She is nurturing, patient, and forgiving. Children seek comfort in her embrace. She is soft and can be manipulated through her deep emotionality in relationship with the less emotional male. Her way of knowing is more intuitive and less objective than man's. She is typically less concerned with *why* than a man. Woman has a spiritual "women's intuition."

In general, men relate with masculine precepts in regard to motivations, desires, and activities. Women generally follow feminine precepts. When we see men and women following contrary spiritual precepts, there is usually a form of spiritual gender dis-identification. This can often be traced back to a dysfunction in the person's primary gender models of childhood.

Chapter Six

Sex, Marriage and Obedience

The physical act of sex between a man and a woman is a natural representation of what is happening in the spirit realm when two become one flesh. "For this reason a man will leave his father and mother and be united to his wife, and they will become one flesh" (Genesis 2:24). Scripture implies that the one-flesh union (i.e., physical sex and the spiritual union of gender) is restricted to marriage.

Marriage is a spiritual construct of promise that embodies all the spiritual laws that lead us toward God and life through love behavior patterns. In the spirit, marriage is a reality of existence between the masculine and the feminine, which together are always as one. In the natural it is a promise between two opposite-gender personalities to relate to each other, connected always by love behavior. Under this covenant we are commanded by God to exercise daily the spiritual laws of fidelity, sacrifice, forgiveness, truth/honesty, goodness, faith, hope, and feminine obedience. God honors marriage and hates divorce (Malachi 2:13—16). God created marriage and even binds Himself by the same laws that He commands of us.

> Later I passed by, when I looked at you and saw that you were old enough for love, I spread the corner of my garment over you and

covered your nakedness. I gave you my solemn oath and entered into a covenant with you, declares the Sovereign Lord, and you became mine.

EZEKIEL 16:8

He states:

Go and proclaim these words toward the north, and say, Return, thou backsliding Israel, saith the Lord; and I will not cause mine anger to fall upon you: for I am *merciful,* and I will not keep anger forever. Only acknowledge thine iniquity, that thou hast transgressed against the Lord thy God, and hast scattered thy ways to the strangers under every green tree, and ye have not obeyed my voice, Turn, O backsliding children, for I am *married* unto you.

JEREMIAH 3:12—14 KJV, EMPHASIS ADDED

So ought men to love their wives as their own bodies. He that loves his wife loves himself.

EPHESIANS 5:28 KJV

Husbands, love your wives, even as Christ also loved the church, and gave himself for it.

EPHESIANS 5:25 KJV

Wives, submit to your husbands, as is fitting in the Lord.

COLOSSIANS 3:18

The church obeys Christ, and wives are commanded to obey their husbands. Disobedience caused the fall of man in the garden. This is a difficult spiritual law for many. Nevertheless, it remains one of the main spiritual laws that have been with us from the beginning. Obedience is a central focus to God and exists as the power-core of commandment. Without obedience, God's commandments lose their power. "If ye love me, keep my commandments" (John 14:15 KJV).

Marriage embodies all the spiritual laws that lead man toward God by commanding certain behavioral attitudes and practices. God attempts to guide us toward life through commandment, which requires obedience. If marriage contains all the spiritual laws, it is to be expected that God would command obedience in marriage.

This is the same principle used by God in relation to Adam and Eve when He commanded them not to eat of the tree. This commandment required obedience. When they disobeyed, their eyes were opened to disobedience and rebellion. They had no idea what disobedience was until they experienced it. With disobedience came all other forms of sin.

They immediately experienced shame.

> But the Lord God called to the man, "Where are you?" He answered, "I heard you in the garden, and I was afraid because I was naked; so I hid." And he said, "Who told you that you were naked? Have you eaten from the tree that I commanded you not to eat from?"
>
> GENESIS 3:9—11

Prior to the fall of man, Adam and his wife were naked and not ashamed (Genesis 2:25 KJV). Disobedience begets shame. Shame begets fear. Adam stated that he was afraid. Fear blocks hope and trust. Lack of hope and trust destroys faith. Without faith it is impossible to please God (Hebrews 11:6) or be completely alive like him. Disobedience is not like God. Sin is death (negative pole) (Romans 6:23).

By one act of disobedience, Adam and Eve became alive to all other forms of spiritual death. "When pride (negative pole) cometh, then cometh shame (negative pole): but with the lowly (humble) is wisdom" (Proverbs 11:2 KJV).

The Lord knew that one negative would draw other negatives. He warned them, "But you must not eat from the tree of the knowledge of good and evil, for when you eat of it you will surely die" (Genesis 2:17). That is like saying, "The day that you disobey, you will learn disobedience and, subsequently, all other facets of spiritual death. These include, shame, guilt, fear, doubt, and lack of faith in Me."

To be like God is to be completely alive, and to be unlike God is to be completely dead.

Commandments are given for our protection, and obedience is the vehicle through which they protect us. Obedience keeps us close to God. "For the commandment is a lamp; and the law is light; and reproofs of instruction are the way of life (the way to God)" (Proverbs 6:23 KJV).

One might ask, "Why didn't God create just one person and give him the balance that exists in Himself? Why is there a need for two created beings showing different spiritual makeups? Why not create man as one, self-sufficient, needing no other? Isn't this the true, perfect image of God? He is God alone and needs no one else."

Herein lies the concept of relationship. God created us male and female in order to require relationship among His creation. But why do we need relationship? God is one. So where is His relationship?

God is actually three in one. He states, "Let us make man in our image" (Genesis 1:26 KJV). This Scripture gives validation to the triune nature of God as Father, Son, and Holy Spirit.

God's nature is love. There must be relationship in order for love to be expressed. God says, in reference to Jesus, "This is my beloved Son, in whom I am well pleased" (Matthew 3:17 KJV). When asked what was the greatest commandment, Jesus states:

> Love the Lord your God with all your heart and with all your soul and with all your mind. This is the first and greatest commandment. And the second is like it: Love your neighbor as yourself. All the Law and the Prophets hang on these two commandments.
>
> MATTHEW 22:37—40

Man and woman were created as two in order to exhibit love in relationship. Everything God does is motivated by love.

"For God so loved the world, that He gave…" (John 3:16 KJV).

"I have loved thee with an everlasting love" (Jeremiah 31:3 KJV).

"For I am persuaded, that neither death, nor life, nor angels, nor principalities, nor powers, nor things present, nor things to come, nor height, nor depth, nor any other creature, shall be able to separate us from the love of God, which is in Christ Jesus our Lord" (Romans 8:38–39 KJV).

"If you love me, you will obey what I command" (John 14:15).

"Whoever has my commands and obeys them, he is the one who loves me" (John 14:21).

Think of God as you read 1 Corinthians chapter 13. Can you not see Him in this? His nature of love depicted in this Scripture is beautiful. As children made in His image, it is expected that He would want us to reflect not only His image (male/female, masculine/feminine) but also His nature, which is love.

Love requires relationship. "Male and female created he them" (Genesis 1:27 KJV). Essentially God said, "They will love each other because they will reflect my nature."

"In this same way, husbands ought to love their wives as their own bodies. He who loves his wife loves himself" (Ephesians 5:28).

"Husbands, love your wives and do not be harsh with them" (Colossians 3:19).

"Husbands, love your wives, just as Christ loved the church and gave himself up for her" (Ephesians 5:25).

"Wives, submit to your husbands, as is fitting in the Lord" (Colossians 3:18).

Why did the Bible not tell the woman to love her husband? Because submission and obedience are acts of love. Jesus says, "If you love me, you will obey what I command" (John 14:15).

The marriage union is a covenant promise, and it is a reflection of God's relationship with His church (the bride of Christ). There is an order to all that God does.

> But I would have you know, that the head of every man is Christ; and the head of the woman is the man; and the head of Christ is God.
>
> 1 Corinthians 11:3 KJV

Man is the head of woman. They rule earth together as equals, but their gender spirituality places them in separate roles in the relationship. The woman should receive her man not only in the physical body, but also in spiritual connectedness and oneness. In this manner, they become one flesh, completely balanced by the masculine and feminine nature that is rooted in God, for we bear his image. Her submission is out of obedience (positive pole). Obedience is a sign of love for God. When a wife submits to her husband, she shows respect for the nature of God as masculine and feminine. She also shows obedience to the order that God has established. This is not man's commandment, but the Lord's.

God said, "If you love me, you will obey what I command" (John 14:15). As a woman submits to her husband, she shows love for God in her obedience. This commandment is rooted in God's plan of order and protection in the family. Given the spiritual precepts of masculinity and femininity, one can understand why God placed femininity in submission to masculinity. Duty-based, focused, mechanical, objective, conquering, commandment-based, masculine strength is classic to the male mind. On this basis alone, it is clear that masculine spirituality is better suited for the role of protection and covering than the feminine.

This commandment is not given for the oppression of woman but for her protection and provision. This is something that true spiritual femininity would welcome and not reject. Furthermore, it is something that true spiritual masculinity would instinctively offer and not withhold.

This balance is supported by the innate motivations of a man in connection with the innate desires of a woman. In this way, men and women receive what is most desirable to each of them individually. Man receives kingship, a job, and purpose while woman receives protection, provision, and security, freeing her for the purpose of the feminine, which is to bring beauty, comfort, nurture, and serenity to the place we call home.

Some women have a hard time with this commandment, especially those whose husbands are abusive, untrustworthy, unloving, etc. Scripture does allow for separation or even divorce under certain circumstances (Matthew 5:32; 1 Corinthians 6:10—11). A woman is free to choose life as a single woman, a separated woman, or a divorced woman. But if a woman chooses of her own free will to marry and stay married to a man, God's commandment is that she submit.

Feminine obedience is a dangerous subject. A man could use this principle toward selfish ends to harm a woman. A woman may mistakenly use this principle to her own peril. We must always remember that Scripture commands the husband first to love his wife. Love entails all elements of the positive pole (e.g., fidelity, sacrifice, humility, goodness, hope, forgiveness, truth, purity). Only after love is established from the masculine toward the feminine should obedience come into the equation. With choice comes power. Apart from these signs of love, a woman should choose separation rather than submission.

The law of gender calls for the feminine to submit to the masculine in obedience. Unlike the modern belief of many, this law does not imply that woman is less than man. It implies that she is equal as a polar opposite. Left is equal to right and up is equal to down. The circular nature of a wedding band shows this concept well. As one moves toward the left he ultimately ends up on the right and vice versa. As one travels east he ultimately ends up in the west.

Obedience in marriage draws the woman into the man and therefore the man into the woman, for femininity has her own requirements that must be met on equal terms. In chapter twelve, "An Equal Offering to Give," I will discuss how the masculine and feminine both require honor, a form of submission, but in different ways.

Man and woman are made in the image of God. The male body is complementary to the female body. He gives and she receives. This is seen in the physical act of sex. Spiritually, the husband gives security through strength and law. The wife receives protection through weakness and obedience. He gives guidance and she receives direction.

Based on how close we are to God, we may feel dismayed by hearing the terms *weakness* and *obedience* mentioned in relation to woman. This is a result of a lie that we all, in some ways, choose to believe. We have lost the true understanding of what it means to be a feminine woman. Most individuals can relate to the concept of a man giving and a woman receiving. This is our God-given spiritual makeup. Feminine spirituality has a power all its own. This will be discussed in greater depth in chapter ten, "Strength of the Feminine."

Every day that a person remains married provides an opportunity for that individual to practice the spiritual laws of God that lead to life. Divorce takes away the opportunity to practice God-like behavior in the relationship. This leads one closer to death than life.

With this understanding, it is now clear why God says, "Marriage should be honored by all, and the marriage bed kept pure" (Hebrews 13:4).

CHAPTER SEVEN

CRISIS OF IDENTITY

GENDER AND IDENTITY

Identity is defined as "all that constitutes the objective reality of a thing, the distinguishing character or personality of an individual, the individual characteristics by which a thing or person is recognized or known" (www.Merriam-Webster.com). It is important to understand this term in reference to the discussion of gender. If one fails to accurately identify a thing, it is impossible to determine how that thing is to be utilized or for what purpose it was created. If one fails to accurately identify an individual personality, it will be impossible to know how one should interact or relate to the personality in question.

    Any personality can only be defined in relationship to another. If we say that an individual is a hermit, we understand him to live, to some degree, in seclusion from society (other individuals). If we say that an individual is a narcissist, we expect that individual to show a pattern of behaviors that involve infatuation and obsession with oneself to the exclusion of others. We could define any personality trait and find that in its definition lies a relationship to another. Understanding this concept sheds light on the importance of understanding one's own personal identity and how it dictates our behaviors in relation to society.

In reference to human beings, we find three areas of identity that serve as the major factors of individual, personal identification. These are gender, race, and family. The "big three" personal identity factors are all immutable. And they all carry extreme emotional consequences for individuals suffering from crises in these areas.

In regard to human identity, gender stands as the most important factor for personal identification. Without a clear understanding of one's gender status, an individual will be at a loss as to where he or she fits in relationship to the rest of the world. Gender identity determines one's behaviors and interactions with other humans. This is true in regard to how one relates to individuals of his or her own gender as well as the opposite one.

When one speaks of an individual personality, it is impossible to describe the person without acknowledging his or her gender. The pronouns *he* and *she* are generic terms used in reference to other human beings. Apart from describing a person by name, gender is the most important quality about an individual.

Even in the area of names, we see the gender divide. Most names are gender specific, while few are used across both genders. Gender influences the way we refer to ourselves. When a person is born, the first question the parents ask is in reference to the gender of the child: "Is it a boy or a girl?" Only after this question is answered can these new parents begin to understand their relationship with the child.

Since God is neither male nor female, why do we refer to Him in the masculine? He is no more a man than He is a woman. This dilemma shows the importance of gender in the realities of humankind. We even ascribe gender realities to personalities that hold no gender status. We have a difficult time understanding any personality without first recognizing the gender thereof.

It is my understanding that God is referred to as "the Father" due to His masculine qualities of ruler, king, provider, protector, governor, giver, and the great "I Am." These are masculine spiritual qualities of God and should only be referred to in the appropriate gender description. He is the ultimate masculine personality and, as such, He is appropriately called "the Father."

He is also the ultimate feminine personality. However, describing Him by a feminine pronoun is inappropriate due to the nature of spiritual femininity, which exists as a receiver in relation to masculine spirituality. Masculinity reigns in the spirit and so is the appropriate gender personality given to God. He is not a man, and it is imperative that we understand this distinction. The limitation of language pushes us into this quandary when we speak of God in the generic, for He has no gender.

SEXUALITY AND CHOICE

Contrary to gay propaganda, sexuality is not an identity. It is a behavioral term that describes the ability to act sexually, without respect to who or what the behavior is directed toward. At any given time, one may feel sexual emotions toward multiple objects of desire. These may include gender personalities (male/female), self-arousal, inanimate objects, smells, visual stimuli, etc.

Human sexuality is the most varied among all living creatures. This is primarily because of the duality of man as a spiritual and physical being. The spiritual nature of man drives us to many forms of human sexual behaviors.

Homosexuality is not an identity. Heterosexuality is not an identity. They are terms that describe what an individual chooses to do in reference to his or her sexual capabilities. Whether one feels driven by homosexuality, heterosexuality, incest, or pedophilia, there is a subsequent choice that must be made.

Feelings do not give us our identities; humankind is capable of feeling all kinds of sexual drives. This is due to the spiritual complexity of mankind. What we see and experience plays a large role in what we feel like doing. When we use our feelings to justify our identity, we choose to believe a lie about who we are as human beings.

This is the error in the thinking of gay propaganda: that how one feels determines what is justifiable behavior. In reality, one chooses to behave according to what he feels at any given time. This makes the homosexual no different from a heterosexual or a pedophile. Feelings may vary greatly from one moment to the next. They are not static, as are gender, race, and family.

If society buys into the lie that states, "Feelings justify one's behavior patterns," our world is on a slippery slope to sexual anarchy and all forms of deviant sexual behavior patterns. Currently, our society has not fallen so far as to accept pedophilia as a normal alternative sexual behavior choice. However, this subclass of deviancy is openly promoted in modern political-interest groups. NAMBLA (North American Man Boy Love Association) supports sexual relations between adult men and male children. The fact that this group is not outlawed shows the growing sickness of American society. We allow what is immoral to masquerade as human rights.

Thirty years ago homosexuality was in the position that NAMBLA is in today. We can see the erosion of American morality as we look with a wide-angle lens over the decades. The gay rights movement is succeeding in changing the moral values of society over time. It is paving the way for polygamy, pedophilia, and all other forms of sexual sins considered unthinkable by generations before.

How has this happened? America is losing her identity as "one nation under God." A growing number of gender personalities have separated themselves from the laws of God and become laws unto themselves. This is spiritual pride at its core. It places the creature above the Creator in reference to behavior.

Those of us who have eyes to see are the only hope for a society such as this. If we keep silent, America will fall. A culture of lawlessness and rebellion will not stand indefinitely. Rebellion is connected to spiritual death, not life.

> This know also, that in the last days perilous times shall come. For men shall be lovers of their own selves, covetous, boasters, proud, blasphemers, disobedient to parents, unthankful, unholy, without natural affection, trucebreakers, false accusers, incontinent, fierce, despisers of those that are good, traitors, heady, high minded, *lovers of pleasures more than lovers of God*...ever learning, and never able to come to the knowledge of the truth.
>
> 2 Timothy 3:1—4, 7 KJV, emphasis added

Homosexuality is, at its core, a crisis of spiritual gender identity. (I will go into this further in the next chapter.) Remember that gender is a physical and spiritual concept. Physically we look a certain way; spiritually, we behave a certain way. This is God's image upon mankind.

God is a God of order. In an ordered universe, spiritual identity should drive behavior, not the other way around. Special-interest groups claim that feelings and behaviors drive a person's identity. This is a lie. Homosexuality is not an identity. It is a choice based on feelings. This is the truth. However, I do not want to underestimate the severity of this issue. The root of homosexual desire lies at the core of a person's spiritual gender identity. This causes terrible distress to individuals afflicted in that regard.

Many churches and professing Christians have done a disservice to individuals who deal with this issue. It is true that one who has chosen homosexual activity can also choose to stop it. This differentiates sexual behavior from true issues of identity. One cannot choose his parents, to be black or white, or his gender status. However, the choice to behave contrary to one's feelings is believed to be impossible in the face of a core crisis of spiritual gender identity. Such a person feels as if he is choosing to be something he is not. In reality, he is only making a behavioral choice, not a decision of being.

Without an appropriate understanding of the key issues surrounding emotional and sexual development, the homosexual is left in a state of unimaginable despair. God loves all mankind. But His heart for the homosexual appears to be lost in the church today. The reasons for this loss of heart are two-fold: indifference and acceptance.

Indifference is often based on ignorance. Lack of understanding and feelings of hopelessness drive some churches to accept homosexuality as a normal form of sexual practice despite the contrary message of Scripture in this regard.

While indifference ignores the homosexual, acceptance deceives him. Both responses lead him down a road of despair, away from the God who loves him and offers healing to the fragile gender image.

In the next chapter, "Homosexuality and Gender Balance," I will discuss how a crisis in spiritual gender identity serves as the foundation for homosexual emotional development.

The subject of homosexuality is controversial and heated due to the fact that its foundation rests upon the most important defining characteristic of human beings: gender. In chapter thirteen, "The Homosexual and Transgendered Mind," I will discuss the concept of gender immutability. This concept creates an insurmountable obstacle for the individual suffering from gender confusion. Immutability is the basis of identity. One does not just wake up one morning and decide to be something that he is not. The only healthy way to understand identity is through acceptance of it.

Many people are troubled by family identity crises. Ask adopted individuals how they felt when they found out the people they'd always thought were their mothers and fathers did not actually share their DNA. No matter how loving and caring the individual's parental substitutes, this knowledge brings with it a void that cries out to be filled. This void may be filled merely by knowing who and where they came from. But for many, seeking a relationship with the biological parent becomes a necessity in order to bring wholeness to the individual's soul. Surrogate family members may be able to soften the blow to a person's emotional development by offering love and sacrifice. If no appropriate substitute is found, this will reinforce the individual's family identity crisis.

Few people suffer from racial identity crises because there is a clear physical manifestation of race in most cases. Furthermore, family and racial community serves to solidify racial identification. However, a racial identity crisis carries with it profound consequences due to the fact that it is shared among a large population base (groups of races) rather than a small number of family members. Furthermore, in many communities, racial mixing tends to blur the lines of the racial divide. This results in a lessening of racial significance across the board.

Gender serves as the basic identity foundation for all mankind. It is the basis for what it means to be a human created in the image of God. "Male and female he created them" (Genesis 1:27). Therefore, a gender identity crisis is the most severe form of identity crisis known to man. Its immutability offers no surrogacy, as in family identity crises. Unlike racial identity crises, its polarity offers no opportunity for mixing in any individual person. There can be no blurring of lines that would annul its significance. If one fails in acceptance or understanding of one's gender assignment, his is a terrible crisis indeed. There will be no surrogacy or softening of the blow. It will strike to the core of a person, all but destroying an individual's normal relating with other gender identities.

The gender divide is impassable. One does not simply cross over, physically or spiritually. Physical crossing is attempted by individuals who claim transgender status. Some go to the point of surgical sex reassignment (transsexual). Others live in cross attire alone (transvestite).

Spiritual crossing is less obvious in this modern age where gender roles are losing recognition as a reality to human existence. I do not believe that men should never exhibit feminine spirituality or vice versa. Gender behavior is fluid in any individual. But men who exhibit primarily feminine spirituality and women who exhibit primarily masculine spirituality are examples of what I consider a crossing of spiritual genders.

Healing of one's gender identity is possible. However, it cannot be accomplished without deep spiritual understanding, introspection, and application of the spiritual principles that lead us toward God and life (e.g., truth, faith, humility, obedience, forgiveness, sacrifice). It is a hallowed and difficult journey. Many attempt the passage and fail. Others, if properly motivated, do fairly well. Given the core identity issues associated with homosexual development, few even attempt to travel this road to gender wholeness.

Ultimately, the likelihood of success will depend on three factors: motivation for change, type and length of involvement in cross-gender behavior, and age. Poorly motivated individuals don't do well. A good result requires the strength of a person's will to succeed.

The type of activity engaged in, coupled with the length of time an individual has lived a certain lifestyle, will play a significant role in the possibility of change. This is true based on the issues surrounding neuroplasticity, addiction physiology, and learned behavior patterns discussed in chapter four, "Human Development."

Homosexuality and Gender Balance

Male Homosexuality

Why is homosexuality a sin? What is wrong with two people loving each other for love's sake alone? The answer to this question is complex.

First, I would like to challenge the statement that love between two men or two women in a spousal relationship is the type of love the Bible speaks of. The psychology of homosexuality is rooted in deficit. Homosexual males typically perceive an internal lack in reference to certain issues of spiritual masculinity. This lack drives them to unite with someone of the same gender in order to make up for the lack they unconsciously sense in themselves.

Puberty is a time of sexual awakening. It is easy to understand why a boy who admires masculinity in others might eventually develop a sexual attraction for that by which he is enamored. He becomes confused and afraid as he notices this internal conflict. He knows the males he has become attracted to are sexually attracted to females. This serves to alienate him more from gender identification. Before, he only felt different compared to other males. Now, with the awakening of his sexual drive, he "knows" he is different.

In confusion, he may take on a false identity that says, "I am homosexual." The previous chapter, "Crisis of Identity," explains why this is an inaccurate belief. This false identity cannot be equal to heterosexuality because it is born out of lack and personal turmoil. Had this individual possessed a sense of masculinity in himself as a child, he would be less likely to be enamored by it in others.

This identification with sameness propels us outward to unite with what we see as our complement. Opposites do attract in nature (e.g., magnets, complementary male/female sex organs). In parallel fashion, they also attract in the spirit (masculine and feminine).

We see this concept in the family as well. Under normal circumstances brothers do not marry sisters. Cousins do not marry cousins. It is not questioned that fathers are not attracted to their daughters and mothers are not attracted to their sons. Though they are male-female opposites, they are the same in family, naturally and spiritually. This precludes sexual arousal and attraction. Sameness should always repel. In Leviticus chapter 18, God gives rules that determine what constitutes unacceptable sexual behavior. All forms of incest, including relatives and in-laws, are forbidden by God. Most individuals possess a sense of sameness with family early on in development in order to preclude enamoration with them in the period of sexual awakening that is adolescence.

The male who develops a secure masculine identity in childhood should take this into adolescence. He is less likely to be attracted to his male peers. Because when he sees them, he sees himself in a mirror. The man who looks at another man sexually does not see the physical or spiritual masculinity in himself. Were he to see this, it would force him to unite with his spiritual other. In reality, this is a woman. When a homosexual male looks at another man sexually, he does not see himself in the mirror; he sees something other than himself. With this comes the possibility of sexual arousal.

The sex drive was created to drive male and female to unite physically as a natural, earthly correlate to the spiritual union described by God as one flesh. With this union comes the possibility of life. God placed the ability to create and give life in the man-woman combination created in His image. This is the bearing of children.

God is the giver of all life and man is created in this image. The sex drive that propels one toward himself is a drive that has gone awry. There are many ways that this could happen.

As children, male boys are generally more focused on other male boys. They prefer them as playmates and companions. They keep themselves separate from girls. We typically hear boys say, "Girls have cooties." The average parents would find it strange if their six-year-old son were playing with a group of girls rather than a group of boys. A preference for same-sex companions is consistent with gender identification, which begins in early childhood. This is the time when children are discovering themselves and where they fit in the world as male and female, the core aspect of a person's identity.

As boys reach adolescence, they are significantly identified with their same self (male peers) in both shared interests and behaviors (masculine precepts). They have had at least twelve to fourteen years to learn self-identification. In relation to a male peer he may think, *That is me*.

At puberty he is faced with and intrigued by the mysterious creature female, whom he had previously rejected. She is not like him in any way. Her body is different. She does different things. Her conversation is not like that of his male peers. She is a mystery to him.

In adolescence this fascination is sexualized. The homosexual male continues his childlike fascination with himself (and other males) because he has not yet identified with who he truly is: a male. He is the adult child who seeks identity with himself in his peers. This is a form of stunted development. To him girls continue to have "cooties." Like the six-year-old boy, he is still focused on uniting with his sameness. He is not sufficiently gender identified in his own eyes to see his other in female. She holds no sexual attraction for him because his focus is still on other males. She remains absent to him because he has not yet seen himself.

Identity needs to be established before one can know what is the natural opposite that should attract. A firm, appropriately established, emotional and spiritual masculine identity is the definition of manhood. Without this, the adolescent male unconsciously begins his search for secondary physical images of masculinity in which to make contact. This unconscious search takes on the form of fascination and preoccupation. In adolescence this is directly connected to one's awakening sexual drives.

By physical images, I mean male stereotypes (for example, football players, athletes, cowboys, policemen, firefighters, muscle men) or male attire (such as tube socks, boxers or briefs, cowboy boots) or any place associated with male activity (like locker rooms, barns, stables, athletic clubs). These are the images of masculinity worshipped by male homosexuals and serve as foci for sexual arousal.

We see a high preoccupation with fetish sexuality in male homosexuals. Fetish-based sexuality accounts for the vast majority of gay pornographic imagery. Hence, instead of feeling like a cowboy, policeman, firefighter, or football player, like his masculine-identified peers, the adolescent boy only admires them from afar. He does not feel that these images of manhood are representative of himself. He believes other males possess something innate to being a man that he doesn't have.

This *something* is intangible and difficult to describe or comprehend. Many describe it as a feeling of difference. The difference is not necessarily a physical one, but the lack of an emotional/spiritual or male-associated identity. This identity should have been modeled to him in the early stages of his development. He should have attained this in childhood through connection with a masculine role model who would have offered him masculinity by example, confirming his own fragile, developing masculine self-image.

For homosexual males, this role model is nonexistent. Many homosexual men had fathers in the home who were physically present but spiritually absent. This type of father offers nothing to the boy in the way of real sacrificial commitment. Or the child may have received nothing from his father due to rejection of the model. Therefore, he is lacking in masculine confidence regarding his place in the world of men.

Due to his lack of self-confidence, his masculine identity is first suspect in his own mind. As this lack of confidence, which affects his visible behavior patterns, is noticed by others, he becomes labeled as queer, different, gay, etc. If he is resilient enough to at least hold fast to a masculine physical appearance, he will be able to escape being labeled by others. But underneath his masculine camouflage, he suffers in silence. His heterosexually developed companions still prefer him as their primary playmate, but they are not enamored by him sexually because they see him as similar to themselves. The homosexually developed male prefers his friends as his primary playmates as well, but with the added complication of sexual attraction. Unconsciously, he sees himself as less masculine (emotionally and/or spiritually, though not necessarily physically).

This silent suffering begins in adolescence, during the sexual awakening. The God-given sex drive that was meant to propel him toward his natural and spiritual complement has turned in on itself. With his sex drive now alive and powerful, he is transformed from a drifting raft to a speedboat capable of moving contrary to the natural direction of the current. At this point he must harness the power of his will alone, to either resist what he internally knows is contrary or choose to allow his sex drive to propel him violently out of control.

This young man has many cards stacked against him. First, his will is immature due to the lack of self-identification. He does not know who he is. Therefore, choice of direction has no primary starting point. On any journey, you must first find out where you are before you can determine how to get where you are going.

Second, the self-sacrifice, self-control, and mature introspection necessary to tame the awakening sex drive is rarely present in an adolescent.

The only other possibility of control could come from another individual. This person would see the child in turmoil and intervene sacrificially. Unfortunately, a deficit of adult love and guidance has contributed to the child's poor self-image and lack of identity. He can be described as an emotional orphan.

Loneliness is one of the most common feelings expressed by homosexual persons. This serves as an emotional trigger that leads many homosexual men to seek sexual connections in bars or other places where gay men look for others with similar deficits for a mutual sexual rendezvous.

In summary, homosexuality is best described as a dysfunctional, reparative drive to obtain primary alignment or identification with one's God-given gender. Homosexual males desire other men not for what they can give sacrificially in love. The desire is based upon what they believe they get; that is, their lost manhood found in the physical image of another man.

The inability to develop appropriate gender identity is rooted in the early home environment. If the child is ill prepared to relate to the world because of a dysfunctional family rearing, this will handicap the child in identification with peers outside the home. Male children test themselves against their peer group. If there is lack of confidence or perceived inner weakness, it is likely born out of dysfunctional modeling of parental behavior. The child has no good concept of who he is; therefore, he will be emotionally handicapped and can hardly be expected to compete with peers who are more socially and internally secure in themselves.

As the child is forced into communion with his peer group, he sees himself as lacking something, or "different." Homosexuals sometimes use this early feeling of difference as proof that they were always homosexual. This, however, is an erroneous conclusion. Children are not mature enough to possess a sexual drive and therefore can claim no sexual identity. The one who says otherwise is motivated by selfishness. This individual is looking to receive something from a child, not to give sacrificially for the child's well-being.

The political group NAMBLA espouses a core belief that children should be allowed to express themselves sexually without being influenced by society toward what is socially considered normal sexual functioning. Their Web page states, "NAMBLA's membership is open to everyone sympathetic to personal freedom. Our goal is to end the oppression of men and boys who have freely chosen mutually consensual relationships."

What six-year-old boy is in need of or capable of consensual sexual fulfillment? This mind-set ultimately and selfishly draws the adult toward pedophilia, one of the sexual sins. NAMBLA is a pedophile organization whose sole purpose is to legalize sexual relationships between adults and children. Their argument centers around the ability of children to give consent in regard to sexual activity with older same-sex individuals.

My heart sinks with the reality of this situation. It distresses me to even think about this topic. However, the reason I wrote this book was to uncover the lies of modern human sexuality, behavior, and identity.

For the homosexual person, the feeling of being different is not a sexual one in early childhood. The child is describing an increased emotional drive to connect and identify with his already fragile developing gender identity. He is in trouble emotionally and developmentally. The increased emotional interest in same-sex individuals serves as an early reparative drive. This strengthens his perception of gender dis-identification. He feels more interested in same-sex persons than his age-appropriate peers.

Homosexuality is not a separate but equal preference, because it is preferred only by males stunted in masculine identification. These males will be less assertive, less confident, more in need of validation from other men, and more inwardly insecure than the average heterosexually developed person. They live in constant fear of rejection if they're found out.

Contrary to gay propaganda, homosexuals are not a minority group as one would consider blacks, Latinos, etc. These racial groups, as they grow in maturity, cease to be ashamed of themselves in light of immature others who see them as less than human. They can develop extraordinary degrees of strength, both emotionally and spiritually, because of their plight in a fallen world. Minority status serves to strengthen them in maturity through adversity.

Many homosexual persons retain their infantile insecurities and fear of those who would reject them. This is a sign of spiritual infantilism. Many remain closeted late in adulthood and sometimes for life. Those who do "come out" often overcompensate by becoming militant and overly confident. They claim "rights" at the expense of others.

This is clearly seen in the homosexual couple who would subject a child to life with "two mommies or daddies" in a world where mother and father is the norm spiritually and naturally. They consciously subject an innocent child to confusion and pain as they grow into adolescence. They say that love is the only thing that matters, but this is not love as Scripture reveals. The Bible says that love does not seek its own desires (1 Corinthians 13:5).

It is selfish to use artificial means to create life and then subject that life to an existence of pain and confusion in the spirit of "I deserve this" or "It is my right." These homosexuals love out of a drive based on what they can get rather than what they can give. This is selfishness disguised as love. This is not mature love, but an infantile temper tantrum that seeks its own wants above those of others or in deference to the needs of another. A homosexual couple will pass this misconception on to any artificial offspring they may have. The harmful consequences of this are innumerable.

This is the childlike nature of homosexually underdeveloped people. They may be outwardly successful in career or image, but their success serves as a mask to hide their inner deficit and brokenness. They can be prone to image worship (e.g., clothing, houses, jobs) and outward displays of success. These too serve as facades behind which the male child lacking spiritual masculinity suffers in silence. They sometimes create an overly aggressive personality to make up for their self-perceived weakness.

In the male homosexual, the masculine reparative drive is driven out of the God-given masculine character to repair by action or exploration. They seek companionship with other men based on what they can get physically or emotionally from the other, not based on what they can give sacrificially, for that would be true love. This can be seen in the extreme possessiveness, insecurity, fear of infidelity, and violence often seen in homosexual relationships.

Some form of manipulation and power struggle underlies many of these relationships. The extreme promiscuity seen in the gay community gives credence to the self-seeking, self-soothing, inward focus of male homosexuals. Self-absorbed addictive behavior, such as compulsive masturbation, is common among gay men. Hence, homosexual men exhibit their God-given gender assignment in the way that their reparative drive shows itself. They are driven outside of themselves to act/do/search/go after other men in order to get something in an immaturely masculine conquest-like mentality.

The gay male sex drive can never be quieted, for it is born out of an inward deficit that will never be fulfilled by sex.

There is a large community of homosexuals that are constantly on the lookout for suitable sexual partners. They become slaves to passion and lust, forever thirsty but never filled. Sex and masturbation becomes habit forming and compulsive. Eventually, it becomes a physical addiction as the brain becomes accustomed to high levels of endorphins (internal, opiate-like substances), neurotransmitters (central nervous system signals), and adrenaline associated with the frequent cyclical highs and lows of orgasm. This drives the man into a cycle of euphoria, withdrawal, and compulsive searching for the next sexual fix. This is sex addiction at its worst.

In his search for the masculine self, this homosexual becomes a slave. In the end, he is still the empty child orphaned years earlier. It is well documented that homosexual persons are disproportionately prone to severe bouts of depression.[5] Gay apologists universally attribute this to social rejection of homosexual persons by society. But the social conflict and turmoil experienced by homosexuals cannot be the sole contributor to the mental illness seen in the gay community at large.

Female Homosexuality

Lesbians are different from gay men. Their reparative drive is born out of a woman's fear of harm from the male, for fear is common to the feminine mind. This will be discussed in depth in chapter eleven under the subtitle "Eve's Fear." Many lesbians were abused sexually as children or experienced some form of masculine harm. A lesbian might even have witnessed her mother being physically abused by her father. The abuse may be verbal or emotional as well.

The young girl who sees her mother being abused may naturally be prone to fear of harm from men. She may then seek comfort and protection with another woman. However, the protection sought is not actually offered by another woman. It is only perceived protection based on the lack of a masculine presence, not the presence of a feminine one.

Lesbians tend to be extremely anti-male in their stance and demeanor. This sentiment is born out of fear and anger. Fear is a common plight of women in our fallen world. The feminine nature to receive, get comfort, feel protection, and base her worth in relationships is clearly seen in this reparative drive.

Lesbianism is more favorably characterized as avoidance of masculinity rather than a desire for femininity. This is unlike the male homosexual, who seeks another man to get something, in exploration and conquest, to obtain masculinity by masculine means. Male homosexuals tend to ignore rather than avoid the feminine based on an extremely male-focused spirituality.

In the end, masculinity is the driving spiritual power for both male homosexuality and lesbian sexuality. The difference is that male homosexuals seek it, while lesbians avoid it. These dysfunctional sexual patterns give insight into the role of masculinity as the governing spiritual pole of gender realities, for it drives normal and abnormal human behavior patterns equally. In the next chapter, "The Father," we will discuss more in depth the role of masculinity as governing, leading, protecting, and conveying heritage.

Balanced Genders

Gender is the balance of God. "Male and female he created them" (Genesis 1:27). Gender is a transcendent concept that we, as created beings, reflect in our physical natures as man and woman. We also reflect this complementary aspect in our spiritual behavior patterns. The natural physical conflict experienced in homosexuality is a reflection of the spiritual conflict of sameness uniting as one.

Opposites attract. This is a divine law established by God in the physical world as well as the spiritual. Homosexuality is a sin because it violates the nature of God as a balanced being (a concept of gender) and a God of order. The physical world is a reflection of spiritual realities.

If the homosexual connection is not ordered spiritually, anyone who participates in a physical form of homosexuality can be expected to harbor underlying emotional and psychological dysfunctions that support their chosen behavioral patterns. Spiritual dysfunction begets physical, emotional, and psychological dysfunctions, for we live in a universe of parallel worlds. I will elaborate on how homosexuality is a choice based in the heart and ordered by the will in chapter fourteen, "The Heart of Man."

Only in God are gender behavior patterns in perfect balance: His mercy (feminine) and His justice (masculine). However, God seeks to model this balance on earth by creating man in His image as male and female. The argument that sex is just a physical act between two consenting adults shows a lack of understanding of what God has communicated to us about sex. Sex is the physical representation in man of a spiritual concept: the union of gender or the behavioral balance patterns of God.

To see sex as an end to itself, used for the purpose of pleasure only, shows the sensual nature of man apart from connection to a higher spiritual purpose. If seen in this light, one can understand why gay apologists have only one argument. No matter what form it takes, the argument comes down to this basic belief: "I feel; therefore, I must be and must do." This person cannot truly know God, for God is not known by feelings, which are physical and worldly. He exists in the spirit, where behavior is supported by purpose, and purpose is supported by truth, and truth is supported by God, because He is the giver of what is true.

God is truth. Truth is the polar twin of a lie. "I do not write to you because you do not know the truth, but because you do know it and because no lie comes from the truth" (1 John 2:21). Truth is connected to God and life. If feelings serve as the basis for behavior, one could make an argument for any sin or deviant sexual behavior pattern (such as bestiality, polygamy, incest, masturbation, fornication, pedophilia) or even compound sexual sins (such as homosexual, pedophilic incest).

Homosexual sex is physically and spiritually dead. Physically, there is no complementary or possibility of creating life. Spiritually it is also dead, lacking in purpose. Separate our existence from purpose and we find all forms of socially deviant behavior patterns, including sexual sins.

[5]See bibliographical references.

Chapter Nine

The Father

God is a God of order, and he has determined that order would be established through family relationships. He set up the order of God-Jesus-Man-Woman (1 Corinthians 11:3). All direction flows in this way. He calls us His children. We are to learn, get direction from, and obey Him. As natural beings, we each have a father. We are to learn, get direction from, and obey him. As it is in heaven, so it is on earth (Matthew 6:10).

The absence of an earthly father is the earthly parallel to God abandoning us as His spiritual children. The difference is that God can make up for earthly and fatherly imperfections.

I believe the lack of direction, steadfastness, stability, and moral direction of today's society is mainly due to a lack of fatherly direction on the earth. Father is not just a person. Father is a position or office assigned by God. A father has the ability to effect change and turn the tide in whatever way he sees fit.

The office of Father is a divine appointment. Anyone can give sperm and create life (the natural side). The spiritual parallel is to lead, give direction, protect, judge, and be the moral compass through which God gives direction to the family. If this position goes unfilled, the family is left without both a natural covering and a spiritual covering.

Though there may not be a person filling the office of Father for a particular family, the office stands nonetheless. It is analogous to the United States of America being without a president. Every four years we look for someone to fill the office. There are safety measures in place for situations such as an unplanned death or assassination of the president. In the event of an assassination, the vice president is sworn into the office of President. If he is unavailable, the Speaker of the House is sworn in. This goes on almost indefinitely. The office of President is so important that even the death of a president does not leave it empty. If only our families would place as much emphasis on the office of Father as our country places on the office of President.

Too many families have no one standing in the office of Father. There may be sons, grandsons, husbands, dads, uncles, and friends. But in many families, no one is standing up to fill the office. Our families are in turmoil because of this. I have heard some call this the fatherless generation. There is no one to lead, guide, give direction, protect, provide, or serve in masculine strength, courage, and God-given authority. This is a generation of men who are mindless, weak-willed, fearful, selfish, without knowledge, untrained, untamed, flighty, without commitment, absent, complacent, unable to see, blind, and lacking in courage.

Our families, which are the God-given units under which we are to rule earth and serve Him, have no president. Consequently, our direction is off. Our protection is weak. Our mothers are weary. Our children are afraid. Our resources are low. Marauders who would molest, kill, steal, and destroy lie in wait at every corner while men forsake the office and leave it empty.

"How can one enter into a strong man's house, and spoil his goods, except he first bind the strong man? And then he will spoil his house" (Matthew 12:29 KJV). This strong man is the father. We can see this clearly in the natural. If a thief enters the house, the father is the natural first line of defense. Not only is the ability to defend, fight, and display strength built into his physical nature as a man, but his spiritual masculinity drives him with the courage it takes to utilize his God-given strength for the purpose of protection.

This has a spiritual parallel. No devil can tear a family apart without incapacitating the first line of defense (position of Father).

A woman and her children who exist without the protection afforded by the position of Father is a devil's playground. The woman may have some masculine capabilities, but she will not be able to fill this role better than her God-given companion.

One can easily see this in the natural with the thief scenario. A woman may be able to put up a good fight. She may even get lucky and win, warding off the intruder. But this would be a surprise outcome, for she is not physically equipped to withstand such an attack. One would naturally look to the stronger and more capable man to take on such a task.

As it is in heaven, so it is on earth. Because of the God-given position of Father, whoever sits in that role will be the spiritual defense of the family. This should be a man, not a woman.

Many women have been forced into this position of Father due to lack of male companionship. This could be due to myriad reasons, including death, abandonment, complacency, or selfishness on the part of the man. Her attempt to fill this position is wearisome and tiring to her feminine soul. She was not created to exist in that position.

Woman is primarily feminine. Feminine spirituality tends naturally to nurture and comfort, not to fight and protect with strength and ferociousness. Though she may fight and may even be fierce, the weariness of the battle will take its toll.

Man, on the other hand, has the power of strength and fight coursing through every fiber of his being. He loves a good fight. Though he may tire, he regains his strength quickly.

A man who has no toil is a man who is emasculated. He will never be happy. He is the flip side of the weary feminine soul who fights a man's battle. His masculine soul is weak, complacent, full of fear, and lacking courage. Without a good cause, what man will sit by and watch while his wife fights (physically, financially, or spiritually)? The man who does is out of touch with his God-given masculinity. He is weak and leads no one. He may use his physical strength to coerce compliance. But his strength is not driven by the character of God, which is love. Love gives. It does not seek its own. His rule is a selfish rule, only maintained by the strength of his physical body and intimidation.

Such a man may dominate women physically because of his confidence in his physical stature in comparison to hers. Rarely will he stand against a man who possesses true spiritual masculinity. For this man will be confident and not afraid. He may see himself as physically weaker than his rival, but his masculine courage, his desire to protect and serve, will propel him forward with all that is within him. His is a truly masculine soul. The former is emotionally weak and offers nothing in the form of self-sacrifice. He is a coward and has no spiritually masculine strength to fight for the protection of those he loves.

True manhood is found in serving. God's man uses his talents, strengths, and capabilities to serve, protect, and provide for those around him (especially his family). He is a man full of true masculinity. It is not his physical appearance that makes him God's man. Rather, his spiritual strength, courage, desire, steadfastness, and self-sacrifice qualifies him to fill the position of Father.

The Bible states, "But if any provide not for his own, and specially for those of his own house, he hath denied the faith, and is worse than an infidel" (1 Timothy 5:8 KJV). Though he may be faster than a speeding bullet, stronger than a locomotive, and able to leap tall buildings in a single bound, he is a far cry from a masculine man. He is physically strong, but this natural superman will use none of those qualities for the protection of his family.

Show me a family with a father who is not only present but active, engaged, involved, interested, watchful, strong, full of courage, a leader, and a giver of direction, and I will show you a family who is secure, well kept, and unafraid. This is not the family in turmoil. A thief will not easily slip in to plunder his house. If family ruin comes, it does not come without a fierce fight, for a true father will not be easily toppled. His eyes are watchful. He is at all times ready to sacrifice himself in deference to the safety of his family.

His children may be a challenge, but they know where the line is drawn. Even a rebellious, loud, and non-submissive wife will bask in the comfort afforded her by this father. Though she may attempt to manipulate him with her clever speech and wit of tongue, there is an underlying fear of his absence. This fear drives her attempts to manipulate his position. She does not trust the person in the position, but unconsciously, she trusts the position. She tries to manipulate the man in order to gain a sense of security. Unconsciously, however, she realizes that the position of Father is not one that she is able to fill.

When faced with a father who displays all the characteristics of masculinity accompanied by the character of love, rebellious children don't rebel long. A non-submissive, boisterous wife will eventually learn to rest. God is a loving, masculine Father. This is how He is to us all (1 Corinthians 13). He is the Father of all fathers. The true love of our heavenly Father breaks down defensive walls. We are to reflect God's image here on earth.

As fathers, we must do our best to give honor to the position we have been placed in by God our Father. Everything we do is passed on. If you had a father who was inept, would not lead, was complacent, weak, and did not protect, it is likely you will reflect this image. We can only do what is modeled for us. Without the knowledge of his spiritual side, where God our Father exists as the supreme example of fatherhood, a son will be handicapped. He will not know his destiny.

The position of Father carries with it the capacity to convey heritage. On the earthly plane, families are named after the father. This is a natural heritage. We are not surprised when children look like their fathers. As a matter of fact, if a child looks nothing like the father when he is born, people will be asking Mother some tough questions.

We also have a spiritual heritage. As we look like our natural fathers in physical appearances, so we look like our spiritual fathers in actions and behaviors. Sin passes from the first Adam. Hence we are all born into sin, modeled before us by our sinful fathers. We do what we see. We must see righteousness in order to do righteousness.

Abraham was called the father of all who believe. "What does the Scripture say? Abraham believed God, and it was credited to him as righteousness" (Romans 4:3). God promised that he would be the father of many nations (Romans 4:18). He is the spiritual father of all who have faith in God.

Satan is also a father. He is the father of all who lie, steal, cheat, etc. Scripture says he was a liar from the beginning. The first lie ever told was told by Satan. The Bible calls him the "father of lies" (John 8:44). His spiritual heritage rests in the hearts of all who lie and deceive. The Bible states, "You belong to your father , the devil, and you want to carry out your father's desire" (John 8:44).

Just as there is a natural heritage that can be seen physically, there is a spiritual heritage that can be seen in actions and deeds. Jesus says that He is the vine and we are the branches (John 15:1—6). "By their fruit you will recognize them" (Matthew 7:16—20). An apple tree will not bear grapes. An orange tree will not bear apples.

The fruits of the spirit are love, peace, joy, longsuffering, gentleness, goodness, faith, meekness, and temperance (Galatians 5:22). These qualities are found in those who are connected to the vine of Jesus Christ. If you are rooted in Him, your fruit will be visible. "If we claim to have fellowship with him yet walk in the darkness, we lie and do not live by the truth" (1 John 1:6).

A person's faith means nothing if it is not coupled with actions consistent with what he claims to believe. "In the same way, faith by itself, if it is not accompanied by action, is dead. But someone will say, 'You have faith; I have deeds.' Show me your faith without deeds, and I will show you my faith by what I do" (James 2:17—18). Don't be deceived by the big talkers. "These people honor me with their lips, but their hearts are far from me" (Matthew 15:8).

"Examine yourselves to see whether you are in the faith; test yourselves" (2 Corinthians 13:5). Your works are an outward manifestation of what is in your heart. This fruit is your spiritual heritage and it comes from your father.

> I tell you the truth, the Son can do nothing by himself; he can do only what he sees his Father doing, because whatever the Father does the Son also does. For the Father loves the Son and shows him

all he does. … For just as the Father raises the dead and gives them life, even so the Son gives life to whom he is pleased to give it.

JOHN 5:19—21

As fathers, we have the monumental task of passing on a good spiritual heritage to our children. This will benefit them from generations to come. Do not take this lightly. You will be the reason your family is either blessed or cursed. You can place a yoke of bondage on the lives of your children and your children's children by what you choose today. They will only do what they see. If you fail in the position of Father, only God will be able to break them free from their sinful heritage.

Love your children enough to fight for them. You will first fight for righteousness before your Father, God, in your personal life. As He molds you into His image and places His spiritual heritage in you, you can model this for your children.

This outward manifestation can be seen by all. This is especially true for children. They have not yet learned to spin reality into something more desirable. This is a concept I call "the Matrix," discussed further in chapter fifteen. They only do what they see. "Train up a child in the way he should go: and when he is old, he will not depart from it" (Proverbs 22:6 KJV).

When God gave me the revelation concerning the office of Father, I was burdened deeply to see the plight of mankind in this day and age, a fatherless generation. The sorrow I feel can be only a fraction of the sadness God knows. When seen in the light of this revelation, my own experience as a child growing up without a father burns like a hot coal in my innermost being.

My prayer is this: God, You are all seeing and all powerful. You are full of love and mercy. Raise up from this generation men who will fill the office You created them to fill. Insert Yourself into their existence. Fill the void that was left when their fathers abandoned their offices and left their sons lost, with no fatherly model to pattern themselves after. Father, I ask that You model to men your masculine strength, courage, protection, steadfastness, watchfulness, endurance, and will to serve with love. Show us men how to be the men You created us to be. We come before You broken and wounded. We give You all of our lack and imperfections. Fill us with Your ability to be the great "I AM." We are in desperate need of a father's love, protection, and guidance. Model this to us spiritually that it may be well with us and our families here on earth. We are wounded. But we are Your men. Make us into fathers who will be dedicated to protecting and serving our families with all spiritual masculinity. This is our spiritual heritage from You. You are our Father. May Your masculine image rest upon us perfectly, showing Your glory. Amen.

CHAPTER TEN

STRENGTH OF THE FEMININE

Woman, though she possesses some masculine qualities, is the primary bearer of feminine qualities. She is more feeling, caring, full of mercy, forgiveness, primarily a receiver, following, and intuitive in knowledge. Her strength is not physical. This was given to her masculine counterpart, man. Her strength is in her ability to reflect the God-like feminine qualities and therefore balance the primarily masculine man. She is equal to him but different. If she becomes too much like him, she will lose her power and God-given strength.

We were created as both natural and spiritual. To look only at the natural and forget about the spiritual warps our sense of equality. To look at man and woman apart from their spiritual nature causes woman to appear weak. She is supposed to submit and follow.

Because the first man and woman fell in the garden, all men and women live in the natural and are daily waking up to the reality of their spiritual natures. This is why most people feel the Bible is sexist by calling for a woman to submit. They are blinded to their true realities. Most women are unaware of their spiritual power, which, if used perfectly, will completely balance man.

What is feminine strength? We usually hear strength spoken of in association with masculinity. But that bias is a reflection of our focus on the physical nature of mankind. The strength of the feminine is found in spiritual form.

How could God be in perfect balance within Himself as male and female if one portion of His image is weaker than the other? On the contrary, feminine spirituality is powerful. What does it mean to be a woman possessing spiritual power? One cannot approach this subject without showing relationship to the masculine.

Before God created Eve, Adam was on earth *doing*. He had communion with God. God even gave Adam a job. "And out of the ground the Lord God formed every beast of the field, and every fowl of the air; and brought them unto Adam to see what he would call them: and whatsoever Adam called every living creature, that was the name thereof" (Genesis 2:19 KJV).

After there was nothing else for Adam to do, God said, "It is not good that the man should be alone" (Genesis 2:18 KJV). What was not good? The Scriptures do not say. But God's solution to create Eve was not an afterthought based on what Adam needed. God did not just wake up and realize that He had done something wrong. She was already planned prior to Adam's creation.

Our God is a God of order. He understands the masculine and feminine relationship. It is placed within the masculine to do, provide, protect, govern, make a way, show physical strength, etc. Adam had to learn to *do* before God could bring His feminine nature into being. Adam had to learn that part of his masculine image would be to serve as a covering for the feminine creature about to be revealed. Eve would be physically weak, emotionally vulnerable, and in need of masculine protection.

What good is strength and courage without something or someone to fight for or to defend? If all were strong, how would one know it without its comparison to weakness? If all were weak, how would one know it without comparison to strength? Yes, strength and weakness need each other. They define each other. Without the other, each ceases to exist.

And so, here comes Eve, physically weak. Adam is going about his daily activities when he turns around and sees God with this beautiful, meek, soft, alluring creature. He must have fallen flat.

This is the first wedding ceremony, where a Father brings His daughter to the awaiting groom. Are not all brides beautiful on their wedding day? Is not the whole ceremony and congregation fixated on the beauty of the bride? Everyone stands for the entry of the bride. This is the unveiling of Eve. She was beautiful to behold and above all of God's creation, the most desirable.

Adam exclaims, "This is now bone of my bones, and flesh of my flesh: she shall be called Woman, because she was taken out of Man" (Genesis 2:23 KJV). Can you see it? She must have been magnificent!

And herein lies the strength of Eve. It is in her magnificent beauty that she becomes desirable to Adam. Spiritual femininity draws the desire of the masculine. And with the masculine comes the strength desired by the feminine. If masculinity holds the power, femininity commands it.

We see this in the physical as well. For centuries woman has been the desire of man. Women parade before men in their best attire to the delight of all who watch. Have you ever seen a rap video without legions of beautiful, scantily clad vivacious women? The focus of the whole scene is a celebration revolving around the beauty of Eve. Women's clothing is designed to accentuate her beautiful body. Her fragrances and perfumes seek to entice the masculine. Her walk and grace of movement is desirable to behold. Oh, yes, Eve was beautiful and most desirable.

There is not only physical beauty. There is spiritual beauty associated with the feminine. Scripture states:

> Your beauty should not come from outward adornment, such as braided hair and the wearing of gold jewelry and fine clothes. Instead, it should be that of your inner-self, the unfading beauty of a gentle and quiet spirit, which is of great worth in God's sight. For this is the way the holy women of the past who put their hope in God used to make themselves beautiful.
>
> 1 PETER 3:3—5

Let's say you have the choice of two beautiful women. You can choose only one as your bride. They are both equal in physical beauty. Just as you think you have made up your mind, the other becomes more alluring. You do not know which to choose.

Then one of them stands and shouts, "Hurry up! Have you made up your mind yet? Please pick me. I'm more beautiful than she is. Look at my hair. Am I not all you ever dreamed I would be?"

Hands on her hips, loud and aggressive, she loses most if not all of her beauty. Like magic, she becomes ugly and undesirable. No man wants her.

After she is done exposing her ugliness, you turn to the other woman. There she sits, quiet, meek, not forceful or trying to control the situation with her tongue and manipulation. She does not even respond to the insults hurled at her by the other woman. She looks at you with enticing, soft, quiet eyes that convey without words her desire to be chosen. The choice is now easy. She was already beautiful, but in relation to the other woman she has become the most beautiful thing you have ever seen.

This is the spiritual element of feminine beauty. The complaining woman lost her desirable status when she revealed her lack of feminine spirituality, which is soft, meek, peaceful, patient, beautiful, and alluring. In masculine *doing*, she attempted to *get* chosen instead of exhibiting feminine patience and waiting to *be* chosen.

Masculinity does not want to be conquered or told, but to conquer and choose based on his ability to get. Men do not want women who are controlling, loud, and always telling them what to do or not to do. Those are masculine qualities that exist in men and are therefore not desirable to him. The man who exists in relationship with a woman in such a capacity has taken on feminine spirituality while she holds the masculine. We all know couples like this. They commonly say "She wears the pants in this family." Opposites will always attract, whether they are masculine males with feminine females or feminine males with masculine females. I speak in terms of spiritual behavior patterns, not physical appearances.

One might say that woman is weak because she is subjected to patience, waiting, silence, etc., while man has all the power of choice. The woman who thinks like this is thinking from a masculine mentality. She would do well to regain her God-given spiritual makeup. This woman would be analogous to a man feeling as if he had no choices and had to sit in silence. That would be a very unhappy man indeed.

This should not be the mind-set from which a woman functions. Like the silent beauty in the above scenario, in her feminine patience, silence, and allure she draws the desire of her mate.

Once a marriage covenant is established, the strength of femininity binds the two people together with the glue-like power of fidelity (positive pole), a God-like behavior innate to feminine spirituality. Infidelity is usually more of a problem for men than for women. Men may possess physical strength, but it is usually a woman who serves as the backbone, steadfast presence, commitment, servitude, the unionizing force in families. Rarely does a woman stand at the altar with the thought, *If this doesn't work, I'll just call it quits.* She is not the one wavering in front of the congregation. She is sure and steadfast in heart, mind, and commitment. She is not afraid of what she chooses.

As with the fidelity of God, a woman possessing feminine spirituality intuitively says from her heart, "Never will I leave you; never will I forsake you" (Hebrews 13:5). Forgiveness, humility, obedience, and fidelity are inherent to feminine spirituality. God has blessed woman with the power of love. Herein lies the strength of the feminine.

Instead of woman trying to get what she wants in masculine strength, all she needs to do is be desirable to the one who has been given masculine strength. That is man. Spiritual masculinity desires spiritual femininity. A woman who is desired can get whatever she wants from a man. Not by *doing* anything, but by *being*.

If she wants to win a war, she doesn't fight. Someone fights for her. More than likely, the one fighting for her is the one who desires her. Ask any man what he would not do for a woman he desires. A man could have everything, but without someone to give it to, it holds no meaning. James Brown sang a song that depicts this concept. He goes on and on for many verses about the accomplishments of men in the earth, and in the chorus he states that we live in a man's world. But that world loses significance without a woman or a girl.

What is a woman to do if she wants something (e.g., a field plowed, a tree chopped, a car fixed, a husband who stays home)? The answer is, nothing. She must simply be desirable to the one whom she expects to receive from. This is how she will *get*: by *being*.

Many women have a hard time with this because they have been failed in so many ways by men they've trusted. Consequently, they attempt to take on the masculine role of doing and getting in order to have. These women are tired souls. They do not remain spiritually beautiful. They lose faith in their God-given feminine image. When a woman loses her feminine image, she loses her strength.

We need to realize a key spiritual point. By getting aggressive, women become less desirable to truly masculine males. After all is said and done, a masculine man is what a woman really wants. The aggressive woman will, undoubtedly, wind up with a feminine man whom she will end up supporting financially. And in the end, she'll nag him about why he doesn't do anything. She doesn't realize that it was her masculine strength that got her that feminine man. She is *doing* and he is *being*. This is classic spiritual role reversal.

Though the relationship may thrive, both will be unhappy. The woman will be unhappy because, deep inside, she wants a man who will handle things for her. She wants a man to offer her protection and security. But she is the one who is handling it and offering security. She becomes tired and frustrated. This eventually turns into anger and resentment.

The man will bask in the luxury of having, but he feels worthless because he knows he has not offered or done anything. His self-esteem will be low and his motivation even lower for fear of failure. This is a spiritually weak man. He offers nothing. He is prone to many forms of sexual addictions and substance-abuse issues.

True spiritual femininity is strong in that it has the ability to frustrate the masculine in light of an inappropriate offering. It is incumbent upon the masculine soul to offer an appropriate gift to the feminine. And it is the choice of the feminine whether to receive or reject.

Here is an example. God, in perfect feminine strength, receives Abel's sacrifice and rejects Cain's (Genesis 4:3—7). In frustration, Cain kills his brother. God then says to him, "Why are you angry? Why is your face downcast? If you do what is right, will you not be accepted?" (Genesis 4:6–7). God is powerfully feminine in that He receives only the best offerings from us. Anything less is rejected. He says, "You will seek me and find me when you seek me with all your heart" (Jeremiah 29:13).

God in feminine strength hides Himself until the truly hungry masculine souls (men or women) seek Him with all they have. God will not allow Himself to be tasted by those who don't truly desire Him. He understands His true worth and beauty. This is the feminine image of God that women should bear in relationships.

Above all else, women are desired by men. However, many women are lacking in feminine strength. They allow themselves to be tasted by men who don't truly desire them and in the end pierce themselves through with many woes. Women are not holding themselves until an appropriate offering comes along. Out of their neediness they let any weak offering suffice.

Accepting inappropriate offerings from men will only teach them that you are an easy win. He doesn't have to work that hard for you. In the end, you are less precious and desirable in his eyes. No man respects this sort of woman. He will only use her for his own selfish desires, and in the end offer her nothing. She is left feeling lonely and rejected. She blames him for being a sorry man. In reality, it was her neediness and lack of feminine strength that opened her up to such a weak offering.

The strength of the feminine lies in her choice to receive or reject. In a marriage proposal, it is the man who asks, and woman has the choice to accept or reject. Without the acceptance of woman, man will have no wife. There will be no wedding. Think of the frustrated male soul who publicly propositions a woman for marriage. The whole world waits for the woman to answer. After a long period of silence she responds, "No." He is shattered and ashamed. This is a powerful position to be in.

Women, herein lies your power. First, be desirable physically and spiritually. Then, in feminine strength, reject all inappropriate offerings. Continue in patience and, like God, wait for the appropriate. Don't be out there putting yourself on display with the clothes you wear and places you go. This will only make it easy for a weak man to find you and offer you weak things. If you accept him, you will be a sad woman in the end. Your feminine strength will have failed you to your own peril. It is not his fault. He is a weak man. Had you been strong in feminine strength, you would have frustrated him when you said to him, "No, I am too precious to receive what you have offered me."

A woman should never ask a man for his hand in marriage. I cannot stress this enough. She will be giving away her feminine strength to receive or reject. Furthermore, had he truly desired her, he would have asked her. If he truly desires her and has no courage to ask, then he is weak, lacking the courage to fight for what he wants.

In the first instance, he does not desire you because he did not fight for you. In the second, he is weak. You don't want either scenario. If he says yes to your proposal, you have no way of knowing how he truly feels about you. It is possible that he could say yes and not really desire you. He may say yes happily but feel ashamed that he was afraid to ask. In either case, he is not a masculine man. You do not want him.

If he says no to your proposal, you experience the pain of rejection. Rejection strikes at the core of a woman's desire to be desirable. Her feminine beauty, rejected? Rejection is like death to a woman. She will only set herself up for disappointment by asking a man to marry her. If she does, she shows her neediness and has no feminine patience, which is there for her own protection.

Yes, woman is weak. But her choice to receive or reject serves as her God-given mechanism of protection apart from covenant in marriage. Even in marriage, this spiritual principle applies. But, for the most part, after covenant has been established, a woman accepts covering from her husband, and in masculine strength, he promises to protect her weakness.

CHAPTER ELEVEN

GENDER INTERDEPENDENCE

THE BALANCE OF GOD

Due to the interdependent natures of the masculine and feminine, there is a dynamic interplay that exists between the two. They need each other to exist. They define each other. Without one, you have no concept of the other.

Gender is a polarity of behavior and response patterns that governs the spiritual universe. Masculine and feminine are polar opposites in relation to human behavior patterns. Gender is the relational homologue to color (black/white), temperature (hot/cold), and direction (up/down). This is a reflection of the balance that exists within God Himself as a relational personality. It is also the foundation of what it means to be made in the image of God. In God all things exist. He alone existed in the beginning. Before light and dark, there was God. Before good and evil, there was God. And before male and female, there was the Lord.

> I form the light, and create darkness: I make peace, and create evil: I the Lord do all these things. Drop down, ye heavens, from above, and let the skies pour down righteousness: let the earth open, and

let them bring forth salvation, and let righteousness spring up together; I the Lord have created it.

ISAIAH 45:7—8 KJV

In the beginning was the Word, and the Word was with God, and the Word was God. The same was in the beginning with God. All things were made by him; and without him was not any thing made that was made.

JOHN 1:1—3 KJV

When the Bible says that we are made in His image, it is speaking of a behavioral, relational image that exists in perfect balance within God Himself (e.g., mercy and justice, receiving and giving, submission and rule). Christ is an example of God's mercy, while hell or separation is an example of His justice. Praise and adoration is an example of God's desire to receive, while "Ask, and it shall be given you; seek, and ye shall find; knock and it shall be opened unto you" (Luke 11:9 KJV) is an example of the Lord as our provider (Jehovah Jireh). The concept of the Trinity serves as an example of submission and rule balanced within the Godhead, which is one.

God is all powerful, so to whom does He submit? In order for this behavioral balance to hold true, there must be submission in the character and behavior patterns of God. I believe this is the reason God revealed Himself as a triune being: Father, Son, and Holy Spirit. The Son models the submission of God to Himself. Jesus states, "For I came down from heaven, not to do mine own will, but the will of him that sent me" (John 6:38 KJV). "For I have not spoken of myself; but the Father which sent me, he gave me a commandment, what I should say, and what I should speak" (John 12:49 KJV). Prior to Jesus' arrest He prayed, "Father, if you are willing, take this cup from me; yet not my will, but yours be done" (Luke 22:42).

Certain religions, mainly Islam, rebut Christianity as a polytheistic religion because of the concept of the Trinity. But if we accept this gender discussion, the Trinity concept is the only way God would be able to show the relational pattern of submission existing as a behavioral pattern within Himself. This is why Jesus states, "I and my Father are one" (John 10:30 KJV). "When he looks at me, he sees the one who sent me" (John 12:45). In reference to the concept of gender, Jesus is revealed as a feminine God in submission, who submits to His masculine self. "I know that his command leads to eternal life. So whatever I say is just what the Father has told me to say" (John 12:50).

To only reveal Himself as a God who rules would have left a portion of His nature (obedience) lost to all creation. Hence, this would obscure His nature as God who reigns (Jehovah Elyon). This goes back to why God placed the tree of the knowledge of good and evil in the garden. In order to teach Adam rule, reign, and kingship, He had to also teach him submission. Without knowing submission, he would have no concept of what it meant to rule.

We are God's children. Adam and Eve would know only what He modeled for them to know. We are not creators as He is a creator, for He creates all things. We can only reflect what we see and are given.

Children do what they see and repeat what they hear. They don't come up with anything on their own. Neither do we as children created by our God. We are a blank slate and must have all things modeled to us, just as our children will learn from their environment.

Children will reflect the behavior patterns of their parents. Many times these behavior patterns are the same ones that caused the parent pain during the time when their parents were functioning as their primary models. If the child is not mature enough to extend true spiritual forgiveness for the lack of love modeled by his parents, he will be prone to repeating the same sins years down the road, after his parents have long since lost the position of primary role model to a young child. Years later the child becomes the parent all over again. (In chapter fifteen, "The Healing of Man," I will revisit this peculiar concept of how spiritual forgiveness blocks transmission of ancestral sins from generation to generation.)

God is the great "I Am" and is capable of modeling and imparting truth to individuals who have had no primary concept of a desirable behavior pattern. This is the exception to the rule that states, "We can only do what we see." This imparting of virgin knowledge is accomplished by a process called "revealing." It is also known as "revelation knowledge." God is able to reveal information about Himself and human nature. He is not limited by what we were shown or not shown in a particular environment. This is a function of His feminine mercy. God is the beginning of all spiritual behaviors considered righteous and perfect, even the ones we only modeled by being fortunate enough to have been exposed to a loving parent-child relationship. There was a beginning to the good patterns of relating passed forward. In the beginning was God.

Eve's Fear

Eve was vulnerable, as is innate to the feminine. She was to follow, submit, and be covered. She needed Adam as the feminine needs the masculine. Satan knew all too well the vulnerability of the feminine. That is why he chose Eve as his target for deception.

> "You will not surely die," the serpent said to the woman. "For God knows that when you eat of it your eyes will be opened, and you will be like God, knowing good and evil."
>
> Genesis 3:4—5

With deception he produced fear in the feminine. What was Eve's fear? That God was not giving her His best, that He was holding out on her, that her vulnerable weakness was being exploited by Him, that He did not have good intentions with regard to her. Is this not the fear that grips women in relationships? This is especially true in relationship to men.

Fear began with deception. But fear in itself would not be enough to cause Eve to sin. God said, "But you must not eat from the tree of the knowledge of good and evil, for when you eat of it you will surely die" (Genesis 2:17). Eve had to eat in order to sin. Satan had no power to force her. He could only use deception in order to get her to eat.

Satan used the truth in a twisted way. He was correct by telling Eve that she would learn about good and evil by eating of the tree. But what he didn't tell her was that she would learn of evil and good through disobedience, which was sin. Disobedience violates the nature of submission, which is found in the Godhead of the Trinity. Disobedience is sin.

Eve and Adam knew no more about goodness than they knew about evil. All they knew was what God had given them: rule and submission. Those were qualities that existed within God Himself. They learned about good and evil through disobedience, which is sin. Through eating, they learned about something God did not give them: disobedience.

Like any parent, God shielded Adam and Eve from what He knew would harm them. He wanted His children to be like Him, knowing only how to do good. Had Eve not disobeyed, she would never have known sin. She would have been able to live with goodness alone through the commandment given, not ever knowing about evil. She could have dismissed the serpent and remained in paradise.

I believe that if Satan had approached Adam, he would have been ignored. I believe this because fear is difficult to produce in the male. Masculine spirituality is duty based. Masculinity is prone to focus on duty and task. This is why men desire work and activity. Adam would have likely held fast to the commandment given by God to not eat.

Feminine spirituality is relational. Feminine doing is always motivated by the underlying desire to receive. Receiving covering, protection, and security as the weaker vessel is the basis of femininity.

Satan called into question Eve's security by twisting the truth in regard to why God gave the commandment for them not to eat of the tree. Had he chosen Adam as the focus for his deception, it is likely that he would have been ignored, because security is something that Adam gives, not receives. It would be difficult to produce fear in someone who offers security rather than receives it.

Fear is still the most common emotion experienced by insecure women: the fear of rejection, not being desired; fear of abandonment, not being wanted; fear of loneliness, not being connected in relationship with Adam; and the fear of lost fidelity.

His strength will not be used to cover me only. I am not the apple of his eye and therefore not guaranteed security from him. These are the thoughts women think. Fear is a natural outcome of this. Though unlike Eve, it does not need to lead woman into sin.

Faith combats fear. Scripture talks about a war going on between the flesh and the spirit (Romans 7:10). Faith is of the spirit and of God. "But without faith it is impossible to please him" (Hebrews 11:6 KJV). Fear is of the flesh or negative polarity of spiritual life. "There is no fear in love. But perfect love drives out fear.... The one who fears is not made perfect in love" (1 John 4:18). Love contains all elements of God and the positive pole of spiritual life. Fear is on the negative side. "For God hath not given us the spirit of fear; but of power, and of love, and of a sound mind" (2 Timothy 1:7 KJV). Faith was all that Adam and Eve knew until Satan produced fear through deception.

We still wrestle with the knowledge that God wanted us not to have. That is the knowledge of good and evil, faith and fear, obedience and rebellion, etc. Having only faith and obedience modeled for us would have made life much easier. This is the way God wanted it. However, knowing disobedience and fear creates a situation where we have to consciously choose righteousness (faith over fear and obedience over disobedience) instead of only knowing it, as it was in the beginning with Adam and Eve. The Scriptures states, "I have set before you life and death, blessing and cursing: therefore choose life" (Deuteronomy 30:19 KJV). For all, faith must be chosen over fear. This is especially true for the woman, who is uniquely susceptible to it.

CHAPTERTWELVE

AN EQUAL OFFERING TO GIVE

Honoring the Masculine

Masculine and feminine are equal, and each is necessary for the existence of the other. Without the other, neither will have what it needs or desires. Both masculine and feminine demand honor, but in different ways. We shall begin with the masculine.

Man has more physical strength and musculature than the woman. His stature is larger. His endurance is better. He gives physically in intercourse: he gives seed for reproduction. In relationship, men want women who are supportive, who give validation, honor, and gratitude for their offering.

No man wants a nagging wife who constantly puts him down and shows no respect for his work and ability to provide. Nothing he does is good enough. She shows no honor in the way she speaks to him and is constantly telling him what he is not. This behavior strikes at the core of what it means to be a masculine doer, provider, protector, etc. Such a man will never be happy or have appropriate self-worth, for this is what masculinity desires and needs.

In order for the masculine to have this, femininity must offer it. Masculinity calls for submission from the feminine. If a man does not feel that he is respected and honored at home, he is prone to find self-worth in another. Many women feel that shaming a man into action will get him to move. All that does is get him to move elsewhere.

Your husband desires your praise and adoration. This is what gives him the desire to offer more. If a man feels as if his offering is not good enough or will be rejected, he will likely stop offering anything to you or offer it elsewhere.

A woman has the power to bring out the best in her husband through encouragement, respect, and adoration. This attitude produces in man a desire to go the extra mile. The message from men to women is clear: "Submit to me and you will receive all that I have and can give."

However, women have a choice in whom they submit to. A woman is uniquely equipped for this task through the power of her intuitive feminine mind. It is important for her own well-being that she choose wisely. Feminine submission honors masculinity.

Honoring the Feminine

We turn now to the feminine. Recall the characteristics of femininity: nurturing, inviting, possessors of beauty and desire, physically weak and in need of covering, motivated by relationship to the masculine who offers protection, physically and emotionally. If femininity must honor masculinity through submission, masculinity must offer equally in return. However, masculine submission to the feminine takes on a different form. For femininity is not motivated by masculine precepts of honor, praise, and conquest. Her weakness calls for security and the understanding that her beauty is desired. The heart's cry of every woman is to be loved, wanted, and fought for. This gives her the security she needs and desires.

In order for the woman to feel security, there must be fidelity. She must feel that the strength and covering of her husband is for her and only her. How can she feel secure with a man who offers his strength, which she needs and desires, to another? Infidelity strikes at the heart of what it means to be feminine, desirable, protected, and covered in love.

Masculine infidelity produces fear in the feminine. The basis of that fear speaks to the core of feminine beauty. "He does not desire my beauty because he does not choose me." This is the plight of every woman unfortunate enough to experience the pain of infidelity. This is the ultimate form of rejection for a woman and probably the most common fear of women in relationships with men.

This should not be misunderstood as dysfunctional possessiveness. In light of feminine weakness, masculine fidelity is what offers ultimate security.

Fidelity also gives direction to masculine strength, thereby increasing masculine ability. A man with one wife and one family is a man with focus. The contrary would be a man with one wife, two mistresses, and five children from three different women. He cannot support any of them very well. His masculine strength is weakened by lack of fidelity. None of his women are secure, and all are probably filled with fear of not being desirable.

These women are weak in feminine strength, for they have accepted less than what is an acceptable offering from the masculine. This results in her own individual turmoil and undoing. These women are always plagued by feelings of insecurity, low self-esteem, and unworthiness. Why else would they choose to be second, third, or even fourth when the heart's desire of every women is to be number one through faithfulness and fidelity? The emotional need for connection in relationship with man has become the Achilles heel of the insecure woman weak in feminine strength.

After the fall in the garden, God spoke to Eve about what disobedience would mean for the fallen feminine in union with the fallen masculine.

> Then the Lord God said to the woman, "What is this you have done? ...I will greatly increase your pains in childbearing; with pain you will give birth to children. Your desire will be for your husband, and he will rule over you."
>
> GENESIS 3:13, 16

The desire God speaks of her is the nature of spiritual femininity. Femininity longs to be covered by and live in connection to the masculine. Most women, if they haven't been wounded in some way by active harm or neglect from the masculine, dream of a day when their knight in shining armor comes and takes them into his world of safety and adventure. Most women dream of their wedding day years before it arrives. It is the spiritual makeup of a woman to desire oneness in connection with the masculine.

This desire is forever the source of feminine fantasy, but is also the biggest source of pain and disappointment of woman in connection with the fallen masculine. True masculinity offers covering, protection, security, and adventure to the feminine. Fallen masculinity offers none of these and leaves the feminine in a perpetual state of wanting and desiring something that will never be offered in a way that is suitable to the innate cries of feminine desire.

The lack of masculine offering toward the feminine does not negate the desire. The need to be wanted, chosen, covered, honored, and adored is the essence of femininity. A woman can only be what she was created to be. She cannot reject what she has been innately given by God.

Many women live in a perpetual state of longing for some masculine personality—a male friend, boyfriend, fiancé, husband, or father figure—who is always, in some way, out of reach, never offering security in the way that is called for in the spirit of feminine desire. It is an aching that can only be experienced by the feminine (man or woman). Eve was the primary human bearer of God's feminine image; therefore, He spoke to her, not Adam, saying, "Your desire will be… (Genesis 3:16).

Both the masculine and feminine must honor each other, but in uniquely different ways. Each side will need to sacrifice something for the other. Men need to restrict their natural desire to explore and offer their strength abroad in order to honor the feminine through fidelity. Women need to sacrifice control in honor of the masculine through submission. There will be times when neither side wants to honor the other. But if there is going to be true oneness, this sacrifice is necessary and good for both parties.

Love is the selfless giving of oneself due to the commitment of preserving or producing value in another. Love is not what you receive, it is what you give. This is the mind-set and foundation that marriage should be based upon. If couples were to learn this, there would be less divorce in the world today.

CHAPTER THIRTEEN

THE HOMOSEXUAL AND TRANSGENDERED MIND

Feminine and masculine are spiritual, behavioral action/response patterns and can rest upon either men or women. It is intuitively understood that women will feel and desire; this is what motivates them. It is odd to see this form of desire, neediness, and want in association with men. Typically, these men lack in confidence. They feel the need to be comforted and offered something from masculinity.

Men who feel this way may experience homosexual attraction at the onset of adolescence. The attraction is directed toward men, in part, because man is the primary bearer of God's masculine offering presence. But it is mainly due to a lack of personal identity in the needy one. Men offer and women receive. A man who is looking to receive emotionally from another individual typically seeks that in other men, not women. Homosexual males experience something odd to truly masculine men: the desire of the feminine.

Masculine men, on the other hand, desire women in a different way. A desire for conquest and ownership of woman completes him. This is not the case with all men, but generally, men are capable of existing in multiple intimate relationships with females. Polygamy is a sin perpetrated by fallen men toward fallen women, not vice versa. Who has ever heard of a wife with multiple husbands? This does not happen because women are primarily feminine in nature, and femininity calls for fidelity.

Generally, women find it difficult to exist in intimate relationships with multiple men. If she does, her true desire is usually for only one of her male companions. Masculinity, on the other hand, calls for submission, conquest, and rule. We are all familiar with the concept of a harem. It is more typical to see men perpetrating non-monogamy than women.

The fact that men possess primarily spiritual masculinity shows in the promiscuity noted in the male homosexual community. Monogamy, though sometimes attempted, is rarely achieved. The fidelity embodied within femininity is foreign to the world of men, heterosexual or homosexual.

Man and woman are capable of possessing both masculine and feminine spirituality, and there will always be some overlap. But the primary spiritual makeup will be in line with the physical gender given by God. This is immutable.

By *spiritual makeup* I mean primary motives, feelings, and desires. Transgendered individuals claim sexual identity contrary to that of their physical makeup. However, this is a sign of their inner confusion and turmoil rather than an empiric spiritual or physical reality.

Male transgendered individuals may succeed in looking like a woman physically, but will never look like a woman spiritually. He will be lacking the complete package, which is a female body connected with feminine spiritual precepts of fidelity, nurture, intuition, submission, relation, and humility. She is all encompassing, a creature of feeling and a well of deep emotions. This combination of physical and spiritual complement is what God called female.

A male transsexual is actually a pseudo-woman, false in regard to physical reality and false with regard to spiritual makeup. Usually, you can see the manliness in certain physical attributes of the individual. Furthermore, you will be able to see the masculine spiritual makeup of the individual with respect to his motivations, feelings, and desires. This leads to the dysfunctional relational patterns seen in the lives of individuals who claim cross-gender status. They try to impersonate women physically without understanding that a woman is more than what she looks like physically.

They justify their cross-gender status by asserting that, inwardly, they always felt like women. But I assert that no man has ever truly felt like a woman including all the complexities thereof.

A true woman is awe inspiring and a wonder to behold. A real man would never choose this cross-gender imposter over a legitimate, God-created woman. With such an abundant supply of innate feminine image bearers, why settle for a poor substitute?

Female transgendered individuals are even more rare. Physically, it is more difficult to create a man out of a woman than vice versa. Furthermore, it is statistically a less common occurrence in females.[6] Transvestites/transsexuals are not ever really any different from their God-given gender. Male transsexuals are merely men with mutilated bodies in female costumes. Male transvestites live in female costume alone. Neither of them will ever experience the true spiritual femininity given to women by God. They will never be women, for only God can create gender. They will forever be men but not men. They will claim womanhood but never truly be women.

The security that comes with knowing one's true identity is lost to such an individual. Identity must first be established before one can know what is the polar opposite that offers compliment and oneness. For transgendered individuals, there will never be ownership of true God-given gender. They live in a world of perpetual confusion and fantasy. Emotionally and spiritually stable-minded individuals cannot understand this to be normal. It is typically tolerated, at best, by most people. As long as individuals in society retain even the slightest form of their God-given identities, this form of spiritual and emotional perversion will never be accepted as normal. This will be true regardless of the political manipulation generally promoted in the homosexual community.

Does a male transgendered individual choose a truly masculine man for a partner? Likely not, for truly masculine men will not choose him. Does he choose a woman? Likely not, because a truly feminine woman will not receive him. The only option is found in another who is equally confused about his identity. This is usually another man. A male transgendered person will typically be seen in connection with other men exhibiting similar forms of emotional and spiritual illness. Hence, they are simply male homosexual relationships.

Trans is a political prefix, not a physical reality. It implies change from one to another. Although confused, in reality, they are still only men. Only the focused, duty-based, non-encompassing masculine mind could be capable of transgender behavior: to see oneself as something you are not.

This form of emotional and spiritual illness does not usually manifest itself in women. The strong endowment of spiritual femininity given to women by God makes this a rare find. The feminine mind is whole and all-encompassing. It is generally incapable of this degree of emotional splitting, which is an extreme form of denial. Homosexual/transgendered behavior is typically manifested in emotionally and spiritually wounded men. A quick review of the statistics surrounding homosexual/transgendered prevalence supports this conclusion.

Alfred Kinsey was an American biologist and professor who founded the Kinsey Institute for Research in Sex, Gender and Reproduction in 1947 at Indiana University. Because of Kinsey's research, many believed that homosexual prevalence approached 10 percent of the population. Interestingly, Kinsey never reported that homosexuals comprised 10 percent of the American population at the time. He reported a number of statistics concerning homosexual behavior noted in a subset of the population. His research was flawed due to the practice of sampling bias. This occurs when a subset of the population is sampled and extrapolated to represent the population as a whole.

Kinsey made many errors in that regard. One is of particular interest in reference to his questioning of sexual practices. He oversampled prison inmates in a degree that was inconsistent with the general population as a whole. This led to the highly inflated statistics of homosexual practices in each category reported.

The definition of homosexuality is difficult to define because it entails more than just sexual behavior. There is also an emotional component to homosexual development. One can have a physical homosexual experience but not necessarily possess homosexual emotional attachments or preoccupation. For this individual, homosexual activity is chosen for non emotional reasons (e.g., secondary gain, experimentation, gaming). It is not psychologically pathologic because its motives are made aware in the conscious mind. This person is unlikely to choose homosexuality as a lifestyle. Furthermore, it is possible to abstain from homosexual activity but maintain a significant preoccupation with same sex attraction emotionally and/or in regard to fantasy.

An individual may possess any combination of the previous scenarios and in differing degrees. However, some level of emotional preoccupation coupled with fantasy is usually necessary prior to making the homosexual diagnosis. Children and adolescents are still undergoing physical, spiritual and emotional maturation. Same sex emotional preoccupation and fantasy that persists well into adulthood is essential before the diagnosis can be confirmed.

Unlike Kinsey's research, more recent studies consistently report the prevalence of homosexuality to be somewhere around 1.5 to 3 percent of the male population. Female homosexuality is noted to be half as prevalent as male.[7]

I speak of homosexual and transgender behavior in the same context because the transgendered mind is, by definition, a severe form of homosexual identity crisis. It takes on the physical form of emotional and spiritual confusion regarding one's God-given gender. I am humbled and in awe of God for revealing to us the truth and reasoning behind this controversial and poorly understood phenomenon of human behavior.

---

[6]See bibliography references.
[7]Stanton L. Jones and Mark A. Yarhouse, *Homosexuality: The Us of Scientific Research in the Church's Moral Debate* (InterVarsity Press, 2000), 31—46.

CHAPTER FOURTEEN

THE HEART OF MAN:

SEAT OF THE SOUL,

COMMANDER OF THE WILL

The heart is deceitful above all things, and desperately wicked: who can know it? I the Lord search the heart. I try the reins, even to give every man according to the fruit of his doings.

JEREMIAH 17:9—10 KJV

But the Lord said to Samuel, "Do not consider his appearance or his height, for I have rejected him. The Lord does not look at the things man looks at. Man looks at the outward appearance, but the Lord looks at the heart."

1 SAMUEL 16:7

Above all else, guard your heart, for it is the wellspring of life.

PROVERBS 4:23

What is the heart of man? We have heard that man has a triune existence. You have probably heard of mind, body, and spirit (or mind, body, and soul). We possess a spirit and are, therefore, connected to the spirit world.

In the natural, the brain is the command center of the body. The brain controls all willful and many unconscious actions in a human being, such as breathing. As the brain controls the body in the natural, so does the heart control the spirit/soul in the spirit realm. It can best be described as the spiritual mind or spiritual brain.

In medicine we speak of a concept called brain death or a vegetative state. This is a state where the brain has ceased to function. It is no longer in charge of willful acts or capable of controlling aspects of bodily function. These individual are dead in the mind/brain but alive in the body. The heart, lungs, and other vital organs continue to function, but only with the assistance of life-support machines. The body will not breathe of its own accord without the brain. Life support, therefore, does the job of the brain by stimulating breathing in a person who is brain dead. These people are only physically alive, artificially. They possess no understanding or ability to communicate or relate to the world around them.

The spiritual counterpart to this is the person who is spiritually dead but physically alive. He is unable to exercise understanding or choices that connect him with God and spiritual life.

All individuals exist in this form in one way or another. However, the extreme example is the sociopath described in chapter one, "Parallel Worlds."

The spiritual mind is dead and the body exists on borrowed life support known as the natural physical life. Natural life is not indefinite and will eventually end if not connected to spiritual life.

Physical death and spiritual death are intimately related. We all possess some form of spiritual death and, therefore, are all moving gradually toward physical death. This is the process of natural aging, with an expected end. When the decision is made to withdraw life support from a person who is brain dead, natural death is the expected result.

In parallel fashion, once the appointed days of natural life are spent, we come face to face with our true state of spiritual death in relationship to God. "And as it is appointed unto man once to die, but after this the judgment" (Hebrews 9:27 KJV).

The heart of man is either capable or incapable of responding to the voice of God. I will use multiple Scriptures to illustrate this concept.

> And I will give them an heart to know me, that I am the Lord: and they shall be my people, and I will be their God: for they shall return unto me with their whole heart.
>
> JEREMIAH 24:7 KJV

> I will give them an undivided heart and put a new spirit in them; I will remove from them their heart of stone and give them a heart of flesh. Then they will follow my decrees and be careful to keep my laws.
>
> EZEKIEL 11:19—20

> But the seed on good soil stands for those with a noble and good heart, who hear the word, retain it, and by persevering produce a crop.
>
> LUKE 8:15

> Oh, that their hearts would be inclined to fear me and keep all my commands always, so that it might go well with them and their children forever!
>
> DEUTERONOMY 5:29

> Thy way and thy doings have procured these things unto thee; This is thy wickedness, because it is bitter, because it reacheth unto thine heart.
>
> JEREMIAH 4:18 KJV

> But they did not listen or pay attention; instead, they followed the stubborn inclinations of their evil hearts. They went backward and not forward.
>
> JEREMIAH 7:24

> The disciples came to him and asked, "Why do you speak to the people in parables?" He replied, "The knowledge of the secrets of the kingdom of heaven has been given to you, but not to them. Whoever has will be given more, and he will have an abundance. Whoever does not have, even what he has will be taken from him. This is why I speak to them in parables: though seeing, they do not see; though hearing, they do not hear or understand. In them is fulfilled the prophecy of Isaiah: You will be ever hearing but never understanding; you will be ever seeing but never perceiving. For this people's heart has become calloused: they hardly hear with their ears, and they have closed their eyes. Otherwise they might see with their eyes, hear with their ears, *understand with their hearts* and turn, and I would heal them. Blessed are your eyes because they see and your ears because they hear."
>
> MATTHEW 13:10—16, EMPHASIS ADDED

Here, Jesus implies that the first step in healing is mediated by understanding at the level of the heart.

The second step, turning toward Him, is only possible after the first. This is action based, an act of the will, supported by spiritual understanding. "Son of man, all my words that I shall speak unto thee receive in thine heart, and hear with thine (spiritual) ears (Ezekiel 3:10 KJV).

This hearing or understanding comes only after God's words are received in the heart. A cold, calloused heart will not understand and therefore will not turn due to pride, the polar twin of humility. Subsequently, healing will not take place. This healing is either emotional (healing of the heart), spiritual (healing of the spirit), or natural (healing of the body).

One form of healing usually begets the other forms. But healing of the spirit usually precedes all other forms of healing. Calloused hearts don't heal primarily due to spiritual issues. There is always an element of spiritual pride in the heart of any individual who rejects God's Word.

On the contrary, spiritual humility produces an environment where God's Word finds a place of rest in the heart of man. Rejection of God's Word in the heart blocks the healing that always comes from truth. "Sanctify them by the truth; your word is truth" (John 17:17).

Sanctification is derived from the Latin verb *sanctificare*, meaning "to set apart for special use or purpose; that is, to make holy or sacred" (www.Dictionary.com). The sanctification of man, which comes from God, is an ongoing process that is cultivated by humility in the heart of man. "Wherefore lay apart all filthiness and superfluity of naughtiness, and receive with meekness the engrafted word, which is able to save your souls" (James 1:21 KJV).

Calloused hearts do not heal because they are full of pride. Pride will not receive because it believes it has all that is needed. Pride does not submit in spiritual obedience. It will not receive the truth that is sent to heal the hearts of men. Without truth, there can be no spiritual or emotional healing.

In order to become more like God, we must not seek the things that make us feel a certain way. We must always seek the truth for the sake of truth alone. Many times the truth will hurt. Spiritual growth is a painful process. There is always a dying to self that accompanies it. Only in humility can a person accept the truth or healing offered by God. "God opposes the proud but gives grace to the humble" (1 Peter 5:5).

The heart determines the motivations and personality of any individual. Out of the seat of the soul (or heart) flows man's actions, behaviors, and belief systems. "Above all else, guard your heart, for it is the wellspring of life" (Proverbs 4:23).

God instructs us to guard our hearts. This implies that the heart is vulnerable and capable of being manipulated. Good hearts may be turned bad and bad hearts may be turned good. This turning of the heart is mediated by what a person allows or disallows via exposure.

This may be willful exposure. "Do not intermarry with them. Do not give your daughters to their sons or take their daughters for your sons, for they will turn your sons away from following me to serve other gods" (Deuteronomy 7:3—4).

The heart is also capable of being turned by God. "The king's heart is in the hand of the Lord; he directs it like a watercourse wherever he pleases. All a man's ways seem right to him, but the Lord weighs the heart" (Proverbs 21:1—2).

Our physical bodies are mere instruments moved by the will, which is directed by the heart. "For as he thinketh in his heart, so is he" (Proverbs 23:7 KJV). What you think and accept in your heart is what you will ultimately do. And what you do determines what you are.

It is not the person who feels like committing adultery who is adulterous. It is the one who does it. Any vice is a thought that begins in the heart. If the thought is entertained long enough, it will eventually manifest itself.

The entertaining of a thought is the definition of lust. It is not the thought itself that causes the manifestation. That thought which is lusted after in the heart is what we ultimately see. The heart is central to the life of any person. Over a period of time, it will move the actions of the individual to submit to its desires. This is done by the ability of the heart to command the will.

The will of man is the ability to exert conscious choice with regard to any given situation, regardless of circumstances. As Christians, we live by faith, not by sight (2 Corinthians 5:7). In other words, we behave based on what we believe, not necessarily on what things look like. Belief and faith can be solid, but circumstances will change.

It is not scriptural to act based on feelings or desire alone. On the Mount of Olives, prior to Jesus' arrest, He prayed, "Father, if you are willing, take this cup from me; yet no my will, but yours be done" (Luke 22:42).

Christians should exercise conscious choice based on what we believe. We should only believe what God speaks, because God only speaks what is true. If we have faith in the truth, we choose behavior that is consistent with that truth. The will then becomes the force through which the heart exerts its influence over a person. The will performs what the heart commands.

Obedience is a component of love. Scripture states, "If ye love me, keep my commandments" (John 14:15 KJV). Obedience is a desire that begins in the heart. The heart ultimately commands the will of any individual. Many people can temporarily will themselves to behave according to certain rules. But in the end, we all do those things we want to do.

The heart of man is central to God. When He speaks to an individual, it is not to the natural mind or understanding that He speaks. The natural mind cannot understand His voice because it is only heard spiritually, for God is spirit. Intellectual reasoning is useless when we speak of understanding and knowing God. "Trust in the Lord with all your heart and lean not on your own understanding; in all your ways acknowledge him, and he will make your paths straight" (Proverbs 3:5—6). He speaks to the seat of the soul/spirit. If the heart is humble and good, He is heard or understood. Thereafter, by an act of the will, He is obeyed. This should be the rule, regardless of what an individual may feel, physically or emotionally.

If the heart is prideful, bad, or calloused, God is not heard. This leaves no leverage for His Word (truth) to combat physical or emotional responses to one's environment. Without His truth acting as a harness to the heart, the will is driven by feelings and circumstances of one's environment and not by allegiance to the word God is always speaking at the deepest level of a person. This is what I call unconscious living or conditioned slavery.

Most people live this way. They make willful choices and decisions, daily acting based on unconsciously held motives, desires, and feelings. Why are there so many unhappy souls today? They are living unconsciously. They choose things they don't really want. Their choices are based on what they feel or think they want.

This can clearly be seen in the battered-woman syndrome. This woman always ends up in relationships with abusive men. Others are able to see the destructive nature of her choices. However, she is unable to see this reality. She is unconscious to the motives that drive her dysfunctional desire to be with men who do not love her. In her heart she is afraid. She is unaware of the fear of not being good enough or desirable enough. Though she may look put together outwardly, she suffers from low self-esteem and fear of abandonment. The longer she remains unconscious to the wounds of the heart, she will find herself serving feelings that lead her down paths of destruction rather than fulfillment.

Emotions are not accurate representations of who we are as human beings. They are not always a reflection of what we truly desire. The heart is the place where life's tragedies make their marks. We cover these wounds through denial and repression. However, the effects of these wounds continue to show themselves in our desires and feelings.

The gospel according to feelings has led many into the pit of despair. This is where we find ourselves after we have done all the things we feel like doing. This is the state of any person who uses feelings as an excuse for his or her behavioral choices. It is what the Scriptures call lasciviousness or licentiousness. *Lasciviousness* is behavior that is based purely on feelings, "especially those of a sexual nature often considered indecent" (www.Dictionary.com). The definition of *licentious* is "sexually unrestrained by law or general morality; lawless; immoral; going beyond customary or proper bounds or limits; disregarding rules" (www.Dictionary.com). Those who know God do not live in such a fashion.

True freedom comes only from self-introspection and reflection. It is here that we uncover the motives of the heart. The action or behavior can be the same for any two individuals. But their motives may be different. These motives cannot be covered by denial, repression, or forgetting of the past. Understanding our motives requires knowledge of truth and personal introspection coupled by much wisdom.

It is in the deep heart that we find our wounds and the genesis of many feelings and desires. Only when a person knows himself to this degree can he consciously choose any behavior. Otherwise, he is living superficially, without understanding of his true self. Were he to undertake the task of discovering himself, he may find that his feelings pull him in one direction but his motives seek to obtain something else.

When a person understands the motives of the heart, he can truly make a conscious choice about his behavior. Once the journey to conscious living begins, we discover a new dimension to humanity. This newness entails the understanding that it is sometimes desirable to will behavior that is contrary to what one feels.

Most people live without understanding the motives of the heart. This includes, but is not limited to, the gay rights movement. On the surface, their cause may appear justified. But when we look under the surface, we find the ugly motives of pride, selfishness, and rebellion. God wants our hearts. "These people honor me with their lips, but their hearts are far from me" (Matthew 15:8).

Desire is not equal to identity if it is forsaken at the level of the heart. The heart commands the will. The will commands one's actions. A man will not continually behave in a way that is inconsistent with the way he perceives himself at the level of the heart. "For as he thinketh in his heart, so is he" (Proverbs 23:7 KJV).

We are not what we feel. We are what we willfully choose to do. We will choose to do those things that we embrace in the heart. Jesus states, "But I tell you that anyone who looks at a woman lustfully has already committed adultery with her in his heart" (Matthew 5:28). Jesus is not saying that having an impure thought makes one an adulterer. But lust is a necessary ingredient. Lust is the active engagement of a thought that would be fleeting had it not willfully been entertained with imagination and fantasy.

Scripture states, "But every man is tempted, when he drawn away of his own lust, and enticed" (James 1:14 KJV). Temptation does not come with a thought alone. Temptation comes when one is drawn away through the active entertainment of a thought. This is an act of the will and is what we call lust. Scripture states, "We demolish arguments and every pretension that sets itself up against the knowledge of God, and we take captive every thought to make it obedient to Christ" (2 Corinthians 10:5). In other words, do not allow impure thoughts to linger. We must either actively subdue them or actively engage them with lust. We do not choose these thoughts and may never be able to determine their origins. Impure thoughts will come, but we can choose what we do with them.

The heart is the beginning of sin made manifest in action. Continued lust in the heart will eventually move a person's will toward action. You don't just wake up one day and fall accidentally into serious forms of sin. When we see individuals caught in lewd forms of sin, this is not a fluke occurrence. That thing has been nourished in the heart for a significant amount of time through lust. "For where your treasure is, there your heart will be also" (Matthew 6:21).

A man is not considered a wife beater just because he feels like hitting his wife. If he chooses based on allegiance to God at the level of the heart to control himself and withhold his hand, he will be called righteous. He is a man of control who chooses what is right. If he chooses to behave lasciviously and strike her, he will be called a wife beater.

Likewise, a man is not considered a homosexual just because he experiences homosexual attractions. If he chooses based on allegiance to God at the level of the heart to exercise self-control and refuse sin, he will be called righteous. He is a man of control who chooses what is right. If he chooses to behave lasciviously and engage sexually with another man based on emotions, he will be called a homosexual.

Only God knows the thoughts that cross the minds and hearts of any individual. Most of us would be ashamed to wear a neon sign that flashed in bright letters every thought or feeling that crosses our minds. If a lustful thought is all it takes to claim identity with a certain feeling, I believe there would be many more adulterers, liars, murderers, thieves, gluttons, lesbians, homosexuals, and even pedophiles.

The gay-rights movement should stop trying to find a gene to explain why they feel a certain way. Genes don't encode feelings as they do phenotypic expressions such as skin color, hair texture, or other aspects of a person's physical features. Genes tell us what we physically look like, not what to do. Doing is a function of the will. It is an unconscious argument to use political rhetoric to justify one's behavior. The conscious person sees past this.

No matter what we choose to believe about our feelings, all behavior is a choice. If we give any validity to this concept of genetic encoding of feelings, we may as well begin looking for the pedophile gene, adulterer gene, sex addict gene, or "I'm attracted to redheads" gene. I've never heard any valid explanation for why homosexual attraction is any different from attraction to any other objective focus of one's sexual feelings. Why then do people focus time and energy looking for a gay gene? This is a sign of the carefully constructed agenda to force something intuitively unnatural upon a society that is failing to stand firm in what is and has always been known to be true. Whatever is not the truth, is a lie.

The gay-rights movement is a social-political movement whose sole purpose is to change societal, cultural, and moral norms of sexuality to make room for a subset of individuals who would have it otherwise.

Feelings are mediated by such a large host of environmental, social, spiritual, and emotional factors. They disregard this fact and focus solely on the search for a genetic reason for homosexual attraction. This shows a lack of desire for discovering the truth about the real causes for one's feelings.

There are books dedicated to the purpose of addressing the genetic theory of homosexuality that do an excellent job of disposing this theory by critical study and use of scientific methods of data analysis. Therefore, I don't feel the need to readdress the specifics of that topic here. As this book is more in line with a spiritual, psycho-social approach to human behavior patterns, I would rather redirect the reader to those resources more suited to the critical analysis of scientific data. (See index.)

Gay activists have forsaken truth in search of justification for a desired behavioral pattern. Herein lies the choice; not in feelings, but in action. There is no rule that states you must do what you feel. Feelings do not supersede behavioral or moral constraints. Basing an argument around one's feelings is analogous to an infantile behavior pattern. Infants have not yet learned moderation or self-control.

As we will see in the next chapter, "The Healing of Man," these individuals are typically unaware of the deep emotional wounds levied at the deep heart due to denial, a form of self-protection. These love wounds are inflicted early in an individual's existence, at a time when all men's hearts are pure, as children.

CHAPTER FIFTEEN

THE HEALING OF MAN

LOVE WOUNDS

> Thou wilt keep him in perfect peace, whose mind is stayed on thee: because he trusteth in thee.
>
> ISAIAH 26:3 KJV

The healing of mankind is available to all. This spiritual and emotional healing is always preceded by truth understood at the level of the deep heart. Our true spiritual identity is rooted in the God-given image bestowed upon humankind. This image brings with it the understanding of who we are. It offers the possibility of becoming like God in relation to how we see ourselves.

God is love. Love is sacrificial. Love is always giving. Love does not seek its own. It is the basis for all the spiritual qualities commanded by God in marriage. Without love, one is incapable of exhibiting any of the God-like qualities (e.g., sacrifice, fidelity, forgiveness). These qualities serve as anchors in the universe of creation.

In a fallen world, God-like qualities of behavior heal, protect, and redeem the world while drawing man more and more into Him. Love is the basis for all spiritual qualities that are rooted in God. God is love, and He is perfect in exhibiting the spiritual qualities that lead one toward life.

He is completely alive. "In him was life; and the life was the light of men" (John 1:4 KJV). This passage of Scripture has hidden meaning. Spiritual light is the ability to see truth and understand spiritual concepts. Darkness is blind to spiritual understanding and truth. If we insert the definition of life and light into the passage, it reads as follows: "In him was behavior on the positive pole; and behavior on this pole was the ability to see truth and understand spiritual concepts of men."

We have spoken of God's image in relation to gender, masculine and feminine behavior/response patterns. We have also spoken of God's image in relationship to Him as a spiritual being. Finally, we bear His image in the way that we feel in response to a world lacking in love. Since God is love, this can be analogous to God without Himself. A world without love is a world in turmoil and pain. It will be lacking in the spiritual qualities that protect, heal, and redeem the earth.

When we do not love God, it hurts Him.

> And now, O Israel, what does the Lord our God ask of you but to fear the Lord your God, to walk in all his ways, to love him, to serve the Lord your God with all your heart and with all your soul.
>
> DEUTERONOMY 10:12

> The Lord saw how great man's wickedness on the earth had become, and that every inclination of the thoughts of his heart was only evil all the time. The Lord was grieved that he had made man on the earth, and his heart was filled with pain.
>
> GENESIS 6:5—6

We feel pain and sadness when love is lost. We are created in God's image to give and receive love, which is the foundation for all God-like behavior. Love is powerful. If exhibited consistently, it produces a reciprocal response. If love is desired, it must first be given. In a world lacking in love, the only sure way to receive it is to first give it, sacrificially. God models love for us in order for us to understand what it means to love. "We love him, because he first loved us" (1 John 4:19 KJV).

God's image is marred by lack of love. Man is made in God's image. Lack of love produces a pain response. This pain response is what I call a "love wound." If God feels pain from lack of love, so do we. This is the nature of man made in His image. The greatest commandments are numbers one and two.

> Love the Lord your God with all your heart and with all your soul and with all your mind. This is the first and greatest commandment. And the second is like it: love your neighbor as yourself. All the Law and the Prophets hang on these two commandments.
>
> MATTHEW 22:37—40

THE MATRIX (DENIAL AND REPRESSION)

We are all alive and vulnerable to the pain response. As children, we instinctively look to others for love in the innocent belief that it will be given. The object of this focus typically rests upon one's parents or any individual primarily responsible for showing the child God-like love patterns through modeled behavior. As one grows and becomes acclimated to living life in a world lacking in love, a form of self-protection from the sting of lost love is created. I call this form of denial the Matrix.

In the movie *The Matrix* the earth has been overrun by machines. Humans have been driven underground in order to survive. The machine world is in need of a constant energy source. Subsequently, they have created an existence where human beings serve as a kind of battery, kept alive in artificial incubator-like containers. Their minds are hardwired to the computer main frame and pictures of a wonderful existence are continuously sent to the mind via computer-generated images. This false world created by the machines helps to ensure the slavery of the human race by blocking the reality of their true existence. They believe they are happily married, have rewarding careers, are raising beautiful children, enjoy a great family life, etc. But in reality, they exist in fluid-filled, battery-like containers fed false images of a reality that does not even really exist.

The free humans are living in a world where the sky has been scorched and the sun is no more. The machines have destroyed the environment in an attempt to maintain control of the human race. Free humans live underground in caves, hiding from computer search-and-destroy machines programmed to annihilate the resistance who have rallied to fight for the freedom of all humanity. Freeing enslaved humans from their artificial existence means awakening them to the reality of the true world, a place in which they previously existed as slaves. This is a world torn by war with machines that keep all of humanity enslaved by means of a lie.

The Matrix is an allegorical depiction of the concept I will now describe. This Matrix is man's ideas and belief patterns concerning his existence. It has been fabricated in order to shield the person from the true reality of life in a world without love. To see life as it truly is would cause significant emotional pain. Existence in the Matrix requires a person to unconsciously overlook the issues surrounding his true existence. This is denial.

The way of the Matrix is to deny reality in order to exist without pain in a world that has not loved you. This takes place over time and is always accompanied by a hardening of the heart. This hardening helps facilitate the blocking of emotional pain.

Children are uniquely susceptible to the development of a matrix-like reality due to the immaturity associated with youth. I will attempt to elaborate on this concept a bit further.

As a little boy grows he learns appropriate behavior patterns in relationship to the world around him. In childhood, humility is a given. Identity is the most fragile in a child. He, in humility, seeks direction and asks questions concerning the world around him.

Gender is a reality of existence that drives self-identity. Identity must be established before one can determine the proper course of direction. Males and females are socially and spiritually programmed to behave a certain way in society. This is what culture and human nature requires because we exist as social and spiritual beings.

Spirituality is based on behavior. And behavior connects us to God through a concept called morality. If one does not learn what is an appropriate, normal social behavior pattern, it is likely that lack of personal identity is the core defect that fuels this form of social dysfunction.

Identity is something we are given. It is bestowed upon us naturally by our parents, and spiritually by the laws of God. An orphan is destined to struggle with personal identity, for he exists as *first* in a world in which he sees no personal beginning. Therefore, choice of direction will have no reference point.

Direction means nothing without a reference point. In any given situation, you must know where you are before a decision can be made as to where you must go or in what direction you are heading. We must learn to live and relate to the world around us in a way that is socially acceptable in order to be considered well adjusted.

Gender is a reality of existence that governs social and spiritual behavior patterns. It is imperative for an individual to develop peace, confidence, and security regarding one's gender. Male children must interact with older men in order to establish connection with their God-given gender in behavior patterns. In essence, young male children take on the masculine behavior patterns seen in others by intimate association with male role models. This is also true for females.

Sacrifice and giving are necessary qualities for any person considered as a model. Male and female children are in need of gender representatives who will sacrificially give of themselves to establish solidarity of identity in these little ones.

A father who does not spend time with or mentor his male child into manhood is showing a lack of love for his son. This young man will be looking to him with expectation to receive something he knows can only be given by his father, not by his mother. He is connected to his father in a way that he intuitively knows is different from his mother. This connection is gender.

He seeks the masculine in his father in order to gain confidence in his own gender identity. A father who does not sacrificially offer himself to his son through constant mentorship and positive interaction will be contributing to a pain response in the child fragile in masculine gender identity. A boy without his father is a sad boy indeed.

If consistently rejected, the boy will eventually learn to exist in a world without his father. To do this healthily, the child would need to offer forgiveness to the father for his lack of love. In order to forgive, one must first show understanding of sin at the level of the heart. For it is from the heart that true God-like forgiveness is born.

Understanding sin in the heart causes a severe form of emotional pain. Spiritual forgiveness is God's remedy for sin and the subsequent pain that always follows. Children are immature and incapable of the deep, spiritual understanding and sacrifice that precedes true godly forgiveness. Consequently, the way in which they deal with spiritual pain caused by sin will not take the form of mature spiritual forgiveness. It will take on the form of denial. They learn to harden their hearts to the pain instead of forgiving it.

Ignoring sin is a way of blocking the pain that accompanies it. This ignoring takes on the form of excuse or making light of the sin. In some cases, there is a complete loss of memory surrounding aspects of one's past. This is called repression of memories. It is always preceded by some traumatic emotional experience. Denial and repression help to block true, heartfelt understanding of sin.

It is amazing to see the degrees of sin perpetrated on children who seemingly have no emotional response to their plight in the dysfunctional world surrounding them. These can be molested children, physically abused children, children who witness domestic violence, or even ignored children. They learn to cope by turning off their hearts, the emotional center of the soul.

Spiritual forgiveness is the true remedy for sin in a fallen world. However, maturity is necessary for such a task, and children are in need of growth, physically and spiritually.

Many times these children's minds go blank when asked about the trauma of their early environments. It is not uncommon for children to forget when asked about details of the past. This is a form of repression commonly exhibited by the immature mind. Though out of the conscious mind, underlying is a festering wound covered by years of repression, denial, and flight from pain. Consequently, mature, godly relating will never be experienced by such an individual because he is not in touch with the reality of his own existence.

As these individuals mature into adulthood, they do not mature spiritually, for denial stunts spiritual growth. It blocks the reckoning with sin that accompanies the spiritually mature. Accordingly, mourning and tears are signs of the heartfelt recognition of sin.

Contrary to the belief of some, crying is not a sign of weakness, but a sign of strength, the strength to face squarely the reality of sin experienced from another or sin committed in regard to another. Individuals unable to mourn from the heart, of which actual tears are a sign, are showing signs of a calloused, blocking mechanism erected around the heart to a painful past they have not yet reckoned with.

To live in denial of one's past dooms an individual to live in denial about one's current behavior patterns. An individual who has not reckoned with the pain of being molested will have no ability to mourn someone else living under the same sin in the present. A man who hasn't spiritually reckoned with the neglect of his father will likely excuse himself for neglecting his children in the present. These are some of the ways in which we repeat the past in the present.

Denial, or the Matrix, helps lock us into a perpetual state of repression concerning our current behavior and dysfunction through blocking understanding of past sins and its subsequent pain. This is a form of stunted spiritual development or spiritual infantilism. These individuals are physically mature but spiritually remain as children, living in pain, denial, and repression. They are likely to repeat the same mistakes of their parents due to lack of insight into their past. It is impossible to change what one does not comprehend.

The Matrix serves to protect us from this heartfelt emotional pain but sentences us to a life of bondage to our past as we repeat the sins of our predecessors in the present. This is one of the ways in which sin is passed on from generation to generation.

All persons will experience some form of lost love in relationship to parental models. We are all flawed in one way or another and so doomed to cause harm and pain by our lack of love toward others. Our own children bear the brunt of our sins. They innocently look to us for love. When we fail to model it perfectly, we expose their innocent hearts to the world of fallen men.

In order to experience true spiritual growth, children must come to grips with the reality of their parents' imperfections and learn to forgive even while feeling the sting of lost love. This requires a dying to self, one's personal feelings, expectations, and desires in relationship to others we expect to receive from. This is the self-sacrifice that precedes true spiritual forgiveness. It no longer is about what the other person did not give you, but what you are able to offer instead. This is growth into adulthood from a spiritual standpoint.

"When I was a child, I spake as a child, I understood as a child, I thought as a child: but when I became a man, I put away childish things" (1 Corinthians 13:11 KJV). Resentment, lack of forgiveness, and denial are forms of spiritual immaturity exhibited by individuals living in the hell of their own emotions. For these persons, there will always be someone else to blame for what did or did not happen to or for them. These are the reasons they use to explain away their dysfunctional patterns of behavior. Their focus, like a child, is on others who are expected to offer them something they feel they need or want.

Spiritual maturity takes responsibility for one's actions, regardless of what others are perceived to be doing or not doing. This individual has grown enough to realize that we are all responsible to God for what we do.

> For we must all appear before the judgement seat of Christ, that each one may receive what is due him for the things done while in the body, whether good or bad.
>
> 2 CORINTHIANS 5:10

> For God shall bring every work into judgment, with every secret thing, whether it be good, or whether it be evil.
>
> ECCLESIASTES 12:14 KJV

Blaming others for our actions will get us nowhere. God cannot be manipulated by blame shifting.

The healing of man is a concept of growing out of immaturity (the hell of negative inner emotions) into a place where we can see, live, and follow the commandments of God. We do this while consciously sacrificing our own sinful wills and desires. We begin to live motivated by what God commands rather than what we feel we want in any given situation. We stop looking to receive from others in order to be fulfilled.

Solidarity, peace, and identity comes from knowing God and His will for us in reference to daily life. Mature individuals do not shrink from conflict within their emotions. This is the way of denial, repression, and the Matrix. They face troubles head on with strength, faith, and confidence in the laws of God that direct our behavior patterns. If it hurts, we accept it and then learn to mourn gracefully.

As spiritual healing begins, there is always a period of pain, inner turmoil, and mourning. This is based on the heart's response to acknowledged sin. Afterward, in maturity, we simply learn to forgive.

In the deep heart we love God's law, and we will ourselves to act accordingly. We learn to live in obedience, not by what we feel or don't feel. Therefore, feelings lose the power to control one's actions or behavior. If feelings are no longer the driving force for behavior and choice, we no longer fear the pain of seeing the world the way it truly is, full of pain and lacking in love. Denial, repression, and the Matrix lose their blocking power because there is no longer fear of the pain response caused by lost love. The inner child begins to face reality without the Matrix as his protector. He must now spiritually grow in love, which entails forgiveness. He does this while learning to live in a world full of pain. God now becomes his Father, Hero, Teacher, Protector, Comforter, Provider, or whatever the inner child feels he has or has not received. In this way the focus is removed from others and God becomes "I Am that I Am" (Exodus 3:14 KJV).

God is able to insert Himself into your existence in order to provide the thing that is lacking in you because it was not modeled for you. Through trust and faith in God's promise to be all things to us, He inserts Himself into our past and present realities to save us from our pain. As we learn to forgive, He covers the sins of others by drawing our focus from them to Himself. We simply let it go.

This is as much an act of the will as any action. We must learn to look up out of our personal situations and see Him. This will always be our way of escape.

In the gospel of St. Matthew, Jesus beckoned to Peter to come out onto the water. He did. But when Peter started to look at the waves and storm, he began to sink. Jesus remarked, "You of little faith, why did you doubt?" (See Matthew 14:28—31.)

Do not look at your circumstances and remain in bitterness, anger, and fear of not receiving whatever it is you feel you will not or have not received. In forgiveness, keep your eyes fixed on Him for your needs, and you will walk on water. In this way you can healthily survive whatever you consider impossible in your life.

Obedience is always the first step to freedom. Subsequent to your obedience, God blesses you with the supernatural, indwelling power to obtain whatever you don't have or to be what you feel you are not. Most people have it all wrong. They feel that if God blesses them with the feelings to support a particular behavioral choice, they will choose righteously. But God is spirit, and feelings are natural/flesh. He is not necessarily concerned with how we may feel at any given moment, though He is the God of all comfort, called "The Comforter" in Scripture (1 Corinthians 1:3; John 14:26). He is mainly concerned with our obedience to His commandments, which are for our own protection.

Only after we become mature enough to live in obedience and self-sacrifice does God's supernatural power become available to change your feelings or whatever situation that may seem impossible to you.

Obedience is always required prior to healing. There are many instances where Jesus healed the sick. On many occasions, they were told to do something first. Their obedience preceded their healing. We must learn to trust in Him for our needs. The beginning of this is sacrifice of the self-will and subsequent obedience to the laws of our God.

Femininity, Mercy, and Forgiveness

During the healing process, it is typical to see individuals experience the pain blocked by years of living in denial about their beginnings. Inevitably, this internal pain is directed toward their parents, the ones responsible for loving the inner child who is now learning to spiritually forgive instead of blocking pain through repression and denial.

There is a pain in letting go. Forgiveness is a form of sacrifice. It entails a dying to self. We are all called to this form of spiritual godliness through the commandment of Him whom we love. "If ye love me, keep my commandments" (John 14:15 KJV).

Through forgiveness we learn to free individuals who were previously the focus of our resentment and pain. In freeing them, we ultimately free ourselves from the hell of self and the emotional pain of living out of our feelings and of lost love.

In spiritual maturity we must learn to free the individuals responsible for causing us pain by not loving us appropriately at a time when we needed love from them. Typically, these perpetrators are only living in the hell of their own emotions through unforgiveness and, hence, incapable of offering sacrificial love to others. These are also wounded ones who have not yet learned to forgive others for causing them their own form of personal pain. Spiritual maturity and growth is not bound by natural age. These wounded parents have not yet grown enough spiritually to learn how to deal effectively with their own love wounds. They are bound by denial, repression, and a Matrix-like reality. They are incapable of offering someone else the very thing they have unconsciously wanted. Understanding this will help you to free this wounded parent and in doing so free yourself.

Deep-seated bitterness and resentment have no place to thrive with true spiritual forgiveness, a form of God-like behavior. This must also be modeled to us. To be capable of true forgiveness, one needs to come to grips with his need for it. But understanding this need is not enough. It must be received and understood at the level of the heart in order to produce the mind of humility that precedes forgiveness of another. Individuals capable of true spiritual forgiveness always, in some form or another, understand their need for it and have received it from someone else. Receiving something that is undeserved produces a softening of the heart. This helps facilitate our forgiveness of others.

Forgiveness is commanded by God for our own well-being. The forgiven individual may never change or be any different from what he has always been. He does not have to change in order to be forgiven. True godly forgiveness frees the wounded person by releasing the emotional pain associated with the wounding of the heart. Forgiveness heals the forgiver, not necessarily the forgiven. Though, if the forgiven is humble, he may develop a softening of the heart that comes with receiving something that is undeserved. This godly humility and softening will be powerful in drawing the forgiven toward true repentance, also born in the heart.

Repentance is also required by God. This is true whether another offers you forgiveness or whether they, in pride and rebellion, choose not to.

The following is a passage of Scripture that warrants some discussion:

> For if you forgive men when they sin against you, your heavenly Father will also forgive you. But if you do not forgive men their sins, your Father will not forgive your sins.
>
> MATTHEW 6:14—15

It appears that forgiveness will not be given by God unless we first forgive others. We learn forgiveness by first experiencing it from someone else. A person who will not forgive is likely not aware of his need for forgiveness. He is usually lacking in true godly humility, which precedes the understanding of one's need for forgiveness. A person who does not understand his need to be forgiven will not ask for it.

If one does not ask God for forgiveness, God is not obligated to give it. "If we confess our sins, he is faithful and just and will forgive us our sins and purify us from all unrighteousness" (1 John 1:9). So then, it is safe to say that those who do not forgive have never actually been forgiven themselves or understood their own need for it. They are therefore incapable of forgiving others.

The truth of this person's spiritual situation can now be seen. His lack of repentance blocks his ability to forgive another. Spiritual pride is always at work in the hearts of unforgiving people.

Pride blocks healing by rendering us incapable of receiving the truth that we are actually the ones in need of forgiveness. The thing that blocks God's forgiveness is not that He will not forgive us but that we refuse to ask. Individuals who don't repent will not understand what it means to be forgiven and will therefore be incapable of forgiving others. Understanding this distinction makes it clear why Jesus stated, "Freely you have received, freely give" (Matthew 10:8).

Receiving is feminine, and humility is God-like behavior. True spiritual femininity is humble, and God-like humility facilitates the receiving that is innate to the feminine. Understanding this explains why women are generally more capable of forgiveness than men are. God's feminine quality of mercy is offered to the world in connection with woman, driven by spiritual humility, a godlike behavior innately associated with feminine spirituality.

To understand this concept is to see a woman and stand in awe of God. She is a mere reflection of who He is in totality: humble, welcoming, full of mercy and forgiveness.

> Come to me, all you who are weary and burdened, and I will give you rest. Take my yoke upon you and learn from me, for I am gentle and *humble* in heart, and you will find rest for your souls. For my yoke is easy and my burden is light.
>
> MATTHEW 11:28—30, EMPHASIS ADDED

The soft, comforting, beautiful, peaceful, welcoming, alluring mercy of God is offered to us in woman. How could life be complete without her? Where is rest without woman? A world without woman is a world without God. If men can learn to see women for who they truly are, that acknowledgment will call forth the God-like masculine qualities of service, covering, protection, giving, action, provision, and sacrifice for such a gift offered to us in woman.

The truly feminine will always receive goodness from the truly masculine. Femininity will receive not by doing anything, but by being what femininity is: simply beautiful.

Eve was a gift to Adam in the beginning. Her legacy rooted in the image of God still fills the earth today. Every woman is God's gift of Himself to the world. He continues to remind us of His forgiveness and mercy every time a little girl, the little feminine, is born into the world.

The healing of man is preceded by and intimately connected to the emotional healing of the heart. Only when the heart is freed from the prison of a calloused existence in an effort to block pain can we once again become as little children, "for of such is the kingdom of heaven" (Matthew 19:14 KJV). We recall an existence of living in a world with trust, expectation, and hope that we will be loved for the sake of love itself. As love is relearned, fear fades and we are freed to believe in goodness again. God now serves as the focus of our trust and expectations, not another wounded human soul. Others are free to be or not to be. We, as children, once again look to our Parent (God the Father) to give us the desires of our hearts.

> If you, then, though your are evil, know how to give good gifts to your children, how much more will your Father in Heaven give good gifts to those who ask him!
>
> MATTHEW 7:11

Our heavenly Father is perfect in love. He is sure not to disappoint you.

Chapter Sixteen

Battle of the Mind

Polarity, Choice, and Sin

Contrary to the belief of many, when I speak of healing, I do not speak of freedom from disordered feelings. Desires, good and bad, are an innate part of human existence after the fall. One would need to exist in the state of the unfallen Adam and Eve in order to experience life free of contrary feelings.

Diseased feelings are a secondary manifestation that results from existing in a world that knows separation from perfect love, the positive pole of God-like behavior patterns. We live in a world where fathers abandon families, where mothers kill their unborn children, where people kill, covet, steal, verbally and physically abuse, neglect, cheat, disobey, lie, lack fidelity, and are selfish and unforgiving. This is a world existing on the negative extreme of spiritual existence. This is a world lacking in love. This is a world of sin. This is where we live and we feel that which we experience.

Our feelings will be a reflection of the mirror in which we see ourselves. That mirror is the life experience of man. With the sin of disobedience, Adam and Eve experienced all the other negative polarities of spiritual behavior patterns. Likewise, we learn fear, pain, loneliness, and other diseased feelings directly related to our experiences in a world that does not know God. This is evidenced by our actions in spiritual behavior. Therefore, feelings should not be used to justify any behavioral choice.

Feelings are variable and may be either positive or negative. We must learn to differentiate between them. In order to be free from diseased feelings, one would need to be removed from this planet altogether, along with every possible human experience. Since this is not possible, we must take up arms and fight, for we are born into a world at war.

The battle is being waged in the spirit. This is a battle between positive and negative, God-like behavior and sin, good and evil. This is what I believe the Bible means by stating that man is born into sin. The common doctrine of innate sin states that man is intrinsically sinful from birth and is destined to fail God. This destiny of failure is attributed to something innately flawed in human beings.

I'm not sure this concept is congruent with the totality of what God reveals to us concerning human existence. In the beginning, He created the world and tells us that all of it was good (Genesis 1). I find it hard to believe that He then made man and goofed. Was our creation not equally as good? Did God create a creature destined to become something other than what He would give them? Did He create man in His image, understanding full well that they could never be like Him? There is something flawed in this reasoning. I think a more accurate explanation is revealed in the Bible. The woman and the man were deceived into disobedience (Genesis 3:13).

This was not an innate failure on the part of our parents, Adam and Eve. They were innocent creatures, mere children in mind and at heart. It was a carefully plotted scheme of Satan to deceive mankind into disobedience. This would be mediated by his understanding of the nature of God's image concerning masculine and feminine spirituality. As they were awakened to the knowledge of good and evil, man had to choose good over evil. This was a choice they were never supposed to make.

With choice comes the possibility of rebellion. Once they were alive to the knowledge of good and evil, choice was born. Sin then became alive to them and they fell. Prior to the experience of willful disobedience, they only knew what they had been given by God. That was ordered behavior called life. Man was, in essence, a perfectly created being endowed with the power of a will.

If the being created was perfect, it stands to reason that the will must have been imperfect. But this is not so. The will is not a personality and thereby may possess nothing good or evil in itself. It is only a thing. The will was not Adam or Eve. They were the possessors of it. The concept of a will implies the existence of two polar extremes. Will implies choice, and choice implies polarity: two options from which we can choose.

The Scriptures state that we are born into sin. This means we were perfectly created but born into a universe at war and given the power of choice. That choice was manipulated by Satan and caused man to experience the negative pole of spiritual behavior patterns: sin. Had Adam and Eve not been deceived, I don't believe they would have been capable of falling, and there would have been no sin for them.

I think we need to rethink what the Bible teaches us about the nature of mankind. It is a lie that human beings are responsible for sin in the earth and therefore should perceive themselves as something to be despised. Humans did not create sin. We simply experienced something that already existed prior to our creation. We were deceived into this sort of experience.

When God created man, He created him in His image, which was perfect. Humans existed as God existed in behaviors and feelings prior to the fall. There was nothing sinful in man. However, man was placed in a universe where there was not only good but evil as well. Unknowingly, Adam and Eve existed perfectly in a polar universe where perfection had a balancing power, the imperfect. God even revealed this concept to His creation. The "knowledge of good and evil" was revealed to Adam and Eve in the form of a tree connected to the power of the will by commandment. The commandment was supported by the God-like behavior pattern of obedience. Had there been no deceit, there would have been no sin for man.

>Whether man has innate sin housed within himself or not will be up to the reader to decide. But I believe Scripture is clear when interpreted correctly.

This concept may give some insight into the destination of the souls born in the world but who died prior to the age of reasoning and understanding. I believe they were innately good, not evil. No one knows the complete mind of God, but we can trust that He will judge accordingly. In the end, all humans who live long enough to attain the age of reason and free choice will need to choose redemption through God's plan of salvation. That plan comes through accepting the sacrifice of Christ for the sin of all humanity.

Whether one believes that humans are intrinsically evil or not is a matter of theology and has nothing to do with one's practical decision to accept forgiveness. By the time an individual reaches the age of reason, he will have become aware of his own sins. This is true whether we believe that sin is innate or that it is modeled from the environment in which we live. However, I believe the discussion is worth having, especially if it reveals to us a truer aspect of what it means to be humans made in the image of God. I believe His image was only good.

The Weapons of War

The war that is being waged in the earth is not being fought in the natural with guns, spears, bullets, etc. It is a war of the spirit. It is the war between selfishness and sacrifice, truth and lie, forgiveness and blame/guilt/shame, fidelity and adultery, obedience and rebellion, good and evil. These are not physical things. They are spiritual concepts. Though you cannot touch them as you could a gun or a sword, they are no less real.

This battle of spiritual polarities is waged in the minds of men who use their wills to choose between the two. Based on our will, we choose action that manifests itself as a physical thing in the earth. Actions are ultimately what we see. We do not always see the battle raging on behind the scene.

As stated earlier, diseased feelings are a natural outcome to existence after the fall. After the experience of sin comes the disordered feelings associated with the negative. No one will escape this. I believe the lack of understanding of this very point leads individuals to pray for God to remove undesirable feelings from them. They may as well have asked God to remove them from the earth and all the experiences thereof. God obviously does not do this. Scripture states, "But every man is tempted, when he is drawn away of his own lust and enticed" (James 1:14 KJV). Even Jesus was led into the wilderness to be tempted by the devil (Matthew 4:8—10).

> For we do not have a high priest who is unable to sympathize with our weaknesses, but we have one who has been tempted in every way, just as we are-yet was without sin.
>
> HEBREWS 4:15

If Jesus was not exempt from temptation, what makes us think we should be? An individual who prays for this is showing a lack of spiritual understanding regarding the concept of sin and the fall.

A good example of this would be the person who experiences homosexual attractions. This is a reality for many individuals for a variety of reasons. We hear the common argument, "I asked God for years to free me from these feelings and He never did. Therefore, I must have been born this way." This is a fatal error in understanding. It is a lie that they have chosen to believe based on lack of spiritual understanding. This is the state of darkness. It is blind to spiritual understanding and truth. Many individuals have turned to a life of homosexuality for this reason alone. This is also true for pedophiles, adulterers, or any other individuals driven to do something based on the way they feel at any given time.

God does not leave us weaponless in this battle. He tells us to fight.

> For our struggle is not against flesh and blood, but against the rulers, against the authorities, against the powers of this dark world and against the spiritual forces of evil in the heavenly realms. Therefore put on the full armor of God, so that when the evil day comes, you may be able to stand your ground, and after you have done everything, to stand. Stand firm then, with the belt of truth buckled around you waist, with the breastplate of righteousness in place, and with your feet fitted with the readiness that comes from the gospel of peace. In addition to all this, take up the shield of faith, with which you can extinguish all the flaming arrows of the

evil one. Take the helmet of salvation and the sword of the Spirit, which is the word (truth) of God.

EPHESIANS 6:12–16

What is the armor that He is speaking of? It has to be a form of spiritual armor. We must learn to wage war against evil in our minds by utilizing the weapons God has provided for us. These weapons are a combination of defensive and offensive.

Notice that the armor is basically the God-like behaviors we have been discussing from the beginning. The shield is called faith. Faith "extinguishes the flaming arrows of the evil one" (Ephesians 6:16). This means that we believe the reports of God, not lies hurled at us by the enemy of our souls. If we do not use faith in God's report, we will be susceptible to believing the lies of Satan. Telling lies is the major way that he gets individuals to doubt God. Choosing to believe a lie is the first step toward personal destruction.

The sword of the spirit is the Word of God, and the Word of God is truth. God can only speak truthfully. "Sanctify them by the truth; your word is truth" (John 17:17). Truth is a spiritual sword. A sword is used to attack. It slices and cuts. Truth attacks lies.

> For the word of God is quick, and powerful, and sharper than any two-edged sword, piercing even to the dividing asunder of soul and spirit, and of the joints and marrow, and is a discerner of the thoughts and intents of the heart. Neither is there any creature that is not manifest in his sight: but all things are naked and opened unto the eyes of him with whom we have to do.
>
> HEBREWS 4:12—13 KJV

We must learn to block lies with our shield, having faith in God's report. We then go on the offensive by speaking truth to the lie and exposing it for what it is. In essence, we block the lie with faith and then destroy it with truth.

The other weapons of our warfare are garments that show our status in the army of the Lord (e.g., the breastplate of righteousness, the helmet of salvation, and communicators of the gospel). Communication of God's Word is essential in this war. We know that "faith comes by hearing the message, and the message is heard through the word of Christ" (Romans 10:17). We must hear His word in order for faith to be generated.

As soldiers in the army of God, we build one another's faith (shield) when we speak the gospel (truth) to our fellow warriors. In this way we strengthen one another in battle. A mature soldier knows that we give no credence to feelings in a world ravaged by sin. We listen to the word our God is always speaking and then march accordingly, blocking, slicing, and speaking the truth of the gospel with every step.

We know that we are in a battle when we learn to suffer in the flesh for the sake of righteousness. Prior to the conscious awakening experienced by accepting God's truth, man merely does what he feels. The suffering that comes with sacrificing oneself is nonexistent. We must learn to suffer in the flesh.

> Therefore, since Christ suffered in his body (flesh), arm yourselves also with the same attitude, because he who has suffered in his body (flesh) is done with sin. As a result, he does not live the rest of his earthly life for evil human desires (the flesh), but rather for the will of God.
>
> 1 PETER 4:1—2

By the flesh, I mean our feelings, emotions, and desires, which are contrary to the commandments of God. The flesh is a reflection of the life experiences of a man born into a war of polarity. This flesh is not the physical body, as is commonly believed by many Christians. The flesh is the negative spiritual pole of man's existence, which wages war against the law of God (positive pole).

> In order that the righteous requirements of the law might be fully met in us, who do not live according to the sinful nature (flesh) but according to the Spirit. Those who live according to the sinful nature (flesh) have their minds set on what that nature desires; but

those who live in accordance with the Spirit have their minds set on what the Spirit desires. The mind of sinful man is death, but the mind controlled by the Spirit is life and peace; the sinful mind is hostile to God. It does not submit to God's law, nor can it do so. Those controlled by the sinful nature (flesh) cannot please God. You, however, are controlled not by the sinful nature (flesh) but by the Spirit.

ROMANS 8:4—9

We must put to death the works of the flesh by living in the spirit, following the laws of God, and utilizing our will to choose Him. "I have set before you life and death, blessing and cursing: therefore choose life" (Deuteronomy 30:19 KJV). This is the war we fight and it is fought in the minds of men. "Faith comes by hearing the message, and the message is heard through the word of Christ" (Romans 10:17). Without faith in what God speaks or without His Word, which is truth, the soldier is doomed, a casualty of war. How can one fight effectively in a war that, to him, does not exist? This question is moot to those who are the walking dead. They cannot see, hear, or understand because they are spiritually dead. They walk in the darkness, not the light.

As for you, you were dead in your transgressions and sins, in which you used to live when you followed the ways of this world and of the ruler of the kingdom of the air, the spirit who is now at work in those who are disobedient. All of us also lived among them at one time, gratifying the cravings of our sinful nature and following its desires and thoughts. Like the rest we were by nature objects of wrath. But because of his great love for us, God, who is rich in mercy, made us alive with Christ even when we were dead in transgressions.

EPHESIANS 2:1—5

Do not ask to be freed from your diseased feelings. Simply choose to believe the truth about who you are and what you are. Then, as an act of the will, choose rightly. It may go against everything you are feeling, but we are not doers of what we feel. We are soldiers who, in spiritual obedience, march according to command.

In the end, God will provide us with the good feelings associated with our choice to live in obedience to Him. You may feel good sometimes and at other times not. Don't place a lot of significance in what you may or may not feel. This is a lie of the enemy. As spiritual warriors in the army of God, we never believe lies.

CHAPTER SEVENTEEN

A Story of Personal Awakening

> For whoever wants to save his life will lose it, but whoever loses his life for me will find it.
>
> MATTHEW 16:25

At this point, I would like to share with you some personal experiences from my life that present practical applications of the concepts presented in this text. I hope you will find these vignettes enlightening in your pursuit of understanding how these concepts apply in your own life.

One would need to spend a significant amount of time in thoughtful introspection and soul searching to successfully recognize the behavior patterns of the fallen image of God in himself. I am no exception. For it is through my own painful journey to spiritual growth that God showed me His true image. In the light of His revealed image, I saw for the first time my own wounded and scarred existence. "Now we see but a poor reflection as in a mirror; then we shall see face to face. Now I know in part; then I shall know fully, even as I am fully known" (1 Corinthians 13:12). In the light of God's truth we will see Him as He is and thus be forced to see ourselves as fallen replicas of the perfect.

Most of us spend the majority of our lives upset and angry about past and present personal losses. These losses can be anything from financial lack or a poverty-like existence, a physical ailment or handicap, being born into slavery of one type or another, or relational losses (e.g., parental, spousal, or other love relationship). These losses are typically the sources of painful and sometimes repressed love wounds.

Armed with the revealed knowledge of God's image, I can look back over my life from early childhood to the present day. My life story is one of extreme loss, loneliness, anguish of heart, addiction, and despair. My life would have definitely ended in suicide or been cut short by some other horrible premature end had God not loved me. "Perverse and foolish oft I strayed, but yet in love he sought me. And on his shoulders gently laid, home rejoicing he brought me."[8]

Opening up one's personal life for all to see is not an easy thing. I do it with the utmost trepidation and obedience to my God, whom I love with all my heart and all my soul. As He laid down His life for me, I now gladly lose mine for His sake. I could not have done it had I not learned spiritual humility and sacrifice from the hands of God Himself. My humility rests in my willingness to bear my nakedness. My sacrifice lies in my desire to bear it in order for others to have hope in a God whose image heals all manner of physical, emotional, and spiritual sickness.

As the Lord reminded me in my darkest hours, so I too will remind the reader, "Behold, I am the Lord, the God of all flesh: is there anything too hard for me?" (Jeremiah 32:27 KJV).

My life started in the early 1970s in a small Midwestern town. I was born to a mother in extreme turmoil and emotional pain. My maternal grandmother died due to complications of a home birth when my mother was seven years of age. My maternal grandfather was an alcoholic, physically and emotionally abusive to my mother. My mother tells me she remembers a time when my grandfather was a loving and strong father whom she adored with all her heart. Whether due to the death of my grandmother or for some other reason, he changed into the person who drove my mother to run away from home at the age of nine for fear of losing her life at the hands of her once-beloved father. She was bounced back and forth between the homes of different relatives due to the violence experienced at the hands of her dad. When my mother was fourteen, he died from complications of chronic alcoholism.

Orphaned and in search of love, at sixteen years old she fell prey to an older man who fathered her first child, my oldest sister. As a single mother, and thus even more vulnerable, she met my father. He married her and gave her four more children, for a total of five: two girls and three boys. I was the firstborn son after my two elder sisters. My mother was nineteen on the day of my birth.

My father, age twenty-three at the time, was also the product of a dysfunctional home. My paternal grandmother and grandfather fought verbally and physically on a daily basis. From what I have been able to gather from discussions with my dad's brother, they were not mere disagreements. Extreme violence marked my father's childhood.

My grandfather left home when my dad was fourteen. When asked about his childhood, my dad claims to have no significant memories until his mid to late teen years. To this day, he is hesitant to discuss any of it. In my endeavor to understand my father, my uncle (Dad's brother) has served as my major source of insight into my father's early life.

I suspect the trauma experienced by my father during the years my grandfather lived at home is the source of a severe form of repression with regard to his childhood. At this time, both of my paternal grandparents are still alive. Outside of superficial cordiality, my dad has no significant relationship with either of them.

My dad's late teen years were marked by extreme explosiveness and violence. These fits of rage were signs of significant emotional instability and lack of self-control, obviously driven by the underlying trauma of his early childhood experiences. At age nineteen he joined the military, only to be discharged a year later, disabled due to what the doctors diagnosed as multiple sclerosis. With the loss of his health, violence was no longer an option for the outlet of emotional pain. Substance abuse became a numbing balm for what violence had once covered.

Until the age of forty, my dad was lost to his family due to addiction, self-indulgence, and the chemical soothing of unresolved love wounds. By the time he started to awaken to his true state, I was seventeen and had never relationally known my father. This fact was especially critical to my personal development because I am my father's firstborn son. Where else would I have learned of my identity and strength as a man if not from him? I am David James IV and my dad is David James III. However, we were connected by name only.

After years of neglect and poor parental modeling behaviors, my name became one of dishonor to me. Only after my awakening was I able to see it as my father intended. He gave me his name because, beneath his cold and distant exterior, he actually loved me. However, as a young boy in need of open displays of affection from his father, I didn't understand this. If I had, I never would have rejected him.

My rejection of my father turned out to be the major source of a gender identity crisis that haunted me for the next thirty years. But spending years in denial, I never knew it.

I was a soft-spoken, reclusive child, a boy of few words. From the day I was born, my mother tells me there was an aura of sadness to my existence. As I grew, I became very introverted and lacked the confidence to interact with my peers outside the home. My parents passed this off as normal for childhood.

I felt awkward and different in social situations. I now know this to be associated with a lack of confidence and personal identity. This was caused by the unintentional neglect of my father, compounded by the presence of an extremely emotional and dominant mother who had taken on a strong masculine persona. She learned to fight in order to protect herself in a world where men did nothing but selfishly take from her and harm her, and in the end offered her nothing.

My mother was an angry woman, prone to violent outbursts, typically directed at my dad. At times her anger was manifested toward her children. My older sisters bore the brunt of her anger but my younger brothers and I were not immune. Some of the beatings we endured at the hands of my mother were terrifying.

My dad was distant and showed little interest in us children. He was too self-absorbed to care about the intricacies of our lives. He rarely cared enough to discipline us. The times when he did discipline us usually centered around situations where he intended to show his dominance. My father's discipline was a selfish rule where strength was used to coerce submission. A loving lesson was rarely the driving force behind his interest in us.

Any of us children would have gladly chosen a beating from my father rather than our mother. Though his hand was hard, his lack of concern guaranteed that his strokes would be few. However, Ma's beatings were driven from deep-seated anger, of which we children were never really the focus. We were only peripheral casualties of a war she waged against the significant men in her life. Her discipline was driven by her desire to appropriately guide us in love, but it was clouded by her anger at men.

Most of her beatings were directed at others, not at the simple mistakes of her young, immature children. In light of her personal life of neglect and abuse by her father, her grandfather, my elder sisters' father, and my father, she had never known the covering, comfort, and protection appropriately offered from the masculine toward the feminine.

Extreme displays of violence were normal in my parents' relationship. They did not dwell together in loving peace, but in the repeated cycles of their childhood existences. They were teenagers living in the hell of their own pasts, not mature enough to understand the sacrifice and freedom of forgiveness. In the end, the very pain they wrestled with was what they inflicted on us children. We were doomed to live life in a war zone where the primary battle was waged between husband and wife. We may as well have been the children of my grandparents.

My earliest childhood memory is actually a pleasant one. I could not have been more than three years of age. I was sitting outside on the steps of the place in which we lived at the time. My father was with me and it was my birthday. He asked me if I knew how old I was. I held up one hand and showed him what I thought was the right number of fingers. He smiled at me, took my hand, and corrected the number.

At this time in my life I was fascinated by my dad, but I recall that he was not home much. I now know that he and Ma had been estranged from each other for some time. He did not live with my mother, my two sisters, and me. To the best of my recollection, my brothers had not yet been born.

I recall one evening when I awakened to find my mother and father lying on the sofa together, sleeping. I felt intrigued by my father's presence. I wanted to get close to him, so I crept up to them on the sofa and nudged myself beside my dad. I must have startled my mother and she awakened. She asked me, "What are you doing?" I felt afraid. Believing that I must have done something wrong, I jumped up and ran back to my bedroom. My father had not noticed the interaction. He was still asleep.

Somehow I knew I was more like Dad than like my mother and sisters. I wanted to be close to him in order to find out what he was all about and therefore understand myself. I decided to try again another time.

Prior to this incident, I recall no adverse feelings toward him. But as time passed, my father became the enemy in my mind.

One night, when I was about six years old, I awakened to the sound of yelling and screaming downstairs. I got up and walked down to the living area, where I saw my father and mother on the sofa. He had her in a headlock, with her head pressed into the couch cushions. I do not recall him actually hitting her, but she was begging him to release her. His demeanor was blank and emotionless, as if he were a robot performing a job commanded of him.

I could not understand why he was holding her against her will. It seemed incredibly terrible and cruel. He said nothing, but continued to restrain her. I walked to the sofa and sat next to them. My oldest sister came downstairs, and my mother asked her to call the police. My father yelled at her to get away from the phone. My sister, crying, told my mother she didn't know the phone number to the police department. My mom yelled out, "911!"

As I sat there in silence, many thoughts ran through my head. I felt sad for my mother and I wanted to help her, but I was powerless against what I felt to be an amazing display of strength and violence by my dad. Under my breath I repeated the phrase, "I hate you."

When the police finally showed up, Dad released Ma. My mother, crying, told them about the ordeal. My father denied the whole thing. He said she was crazy and that he never touched her.

I wondered why he would lie. Under my breath, I said, "I hate you and I will never be like you."

From that point on, my father was no longer the object of my desire. I rejected him as my model and began to build a wall against him. I decided that he would mean nothing to me. Though he continued to live with us, I lost all interest in him. He became invisible to me. It no longer mattered to me whether he lived with us or not. After this incident I sided with my mom on every argument or fight they had, though never out loud. I hated my father and secretly wished him harm.

This traumatic experience was a landmark in my emotional development. After that incident, I began to recognize a distinct interest in older males. This was not a sexual interest, as I was only about six years old. It was merely a desire to connect with and be close to an older male figure who was not my father.

This incident brought with it a distinct shift of my focus from dad to any other man who would show me attention. Unfortunately, this neediness led to my first experience of sexual molestation by an older friend of the family.

Around this time many individuals came in and out of our lives. Our extended family was fairly large, and we frequently spent long periods of time living with our cousins or they with us.

One evening, when my siblings and I were taking our nightly baths, a well-known acquaintance of the family, about sixteen years old, noticed me nudging close to him, similar to the couch incident with my dad. I recall having the same interest and fascination that I'd had with regard to my father about two to three years earlier on the night when he and Mother were asleep on the sofa.

Later that evening this teenaged acquaintance molested me.

I felt extremely conflicted about the situation. Here was a man showing me attention and affection, but I did not feel right about the scenario. I felt like an innocent bystander, not actively engaged or participating in the activity.

When we were at my aunt's house, he took me to a secluded place where he molested me again. Whenever we were in a room full of people, he would look at me in a certain way, then leave the room. I knew that was my cue to follow him to a secret place where the deed would happen.

The molestations continued for some time, though I am not sure how long. I started feeling dirty and saddened by the activity, and I felt a strong desire to be free from this individual.

One evening, he signaled for me to follow him. I didn't want to go, but I felt that I could not refuse him. So I followed him to the basement of my aunt's house. Dirty laundry lay scattered about the floor. He undressed himself and lay down on the floor, waiting for me to do the same. I simply stood there with my head bowed and my hands clasped in front of my genital area.

"Don't you want to do this anymore?" he asked.

Without looking at him I shook my head. He got up, dressed himself, and left me there in the basement. I wondered what this would mean for the future, but he never touched me again after that.

Around this time I began hitting myself at school. I recall sitting in class repeatedly slapping myself while my teacher was in front of the classroom. After a while, she turned to me and said, "David, stop hitting yourself." I was not aware that anyone had noticed or that I was doing anything inappropriate.

I must have been in second grade at the time, because shortly thereafter, we moved to the home where my parents still reside today. My teacher told my parents she recommended I repeat the second grade. When they asked why, she stated that I was quiet and did not talk or interact with others in the class. I was socially underdeveloped.

My father asked if I could do the work, and she said yes. He told her I did not have to talk if I didn't want to and insisted that I be allowed to proceed to the third grade. Prior to the start of the next school year, I was sent to a testing center where my academic skills were evaluated. It was concluded that I could do the work, so I started third grade as my dad insisted.

As I grew older, my social capabilities continued to be somewhat impaired with regard to my peers outside of home. It has long been a tradition for the boys in our family to play football. My father took the position of coach for the team I would be a part of. He wanted me to play tailback. However, I lacked the confidence to perform on the level with boys my own age. Though physically capable, mentally I was afraid because

I felt different from them. They appeared to possess something I did not feel I had: a certainty that they belonged on that football team.

In one football game, my father called a play, expecting that I would perform it. But when he looked around, he found me sitting on the bench, away from all the activity. Without a word, he looked at me and then looked away. The game went on without me.

I felt like I had let him down. I did not feel I was the son he wanted me to be. In my mind, I was a failure. We never spoke one on one about the incident. But it became the focus of jokes told about me at family gatherings. This solidified my already poor self-esteem.

My mother started attending a church where she apparently found the Lord. She went on a regular basis and routinely took my siblings and me along. At this point I had no significant consciousness of God or His existence as a personal Being who would walk with me, talk with me, and be my friend.

On the night that I met Him, my siblings, my mother, and I were sitting in a worship service. The pastor started singing a beautiful song. I felt an electricity in the room, a sort of silent humming sound, not heard with my physical ears but nonetheless heard all the same. It was as if something unseen was in the room with all of us, glorious and awe inspiring.

Sitting next to my mother, I began weeping uncontrollably. She looked at me and asked what was wrong. I shrugged. I didn't know. I was simply overcome with emotion.

She asked me if I wanted to go up to the altar and ask God to come into my life. I knew this was what it meant to get saved or receive God into my heart. I also knew it was an act of the will, a choice one makes. It was not a given, for God does not force Himself on anyone.

I was sure God was responsible for the atmosphere in this place, and I felt loved for the first time in my life. I nodded. Mom took me up to the altar, and I asked God to be my Lord.

Afterward, I felt great. I had the feeling that somehow all would be well with me. Though I had just met Him, I had the earnest expectation that I would learn more about Him as time went on. He became my new invisible friend, who would always be there, no matter where I was.

As I learned about God and what He was all about, I discovered His promises to be with me always, to comfort me, even to heal my physical body. I believed all these things. It was like the answer to all my loneliness. I began having personal experiences where I would pray for simple things, typical of what a child would pray for, and receive them almost immediately.

Once I had a stomach ache, and I recalled that God promised to heal our sicknesses. So I went to a quiet place in my bedroom, shut the door, and prayed, "Lord, please heal my stomach ache." No sooner than I asked, a warm feeling started in my chest and made its way down to my abdomen, completely removing all traces of pain as it passed over me. I simply smiled, said thank you, and left the room to continue with whatever I was doing at the time. I was not surprised that this happened because I completely believed that He would do the things He said. I had the faith of a child. "For of such is the kingdom of heaven" (Matthew 19:14). He was my friend and He loved me.

Soon I began to get praise from my mother for my capabilities at school, for I was certainly gifted in that regard. My dad seemed unconcerned about my academic achievements. I was still not the kind of tailback who would make him proud. I began to derive my significance from academic praise rather than in athletics, where I felt awkward and without confidence. This strengthened my connection to my mother and distanced me further from identifying with my father.

Unfortunately, this personal victory was short lived. I continued to lack social skills. My mother and sister taunted me with the fact that I was academically smart but possessed no "mother wit." This angered me, but they would not be convinced otherwise. Their words were a crushing blow to my self-esteem. I felt doomed to be a simpleton. Not even my scholastic aptitude could rescue me from my apparent inadequacies.

When I started eighth grade, at the age of thirteen, this was the beginning of puberty for me. Though still unsure of myself socially, my physical giftedness began to show itself in relationship to the other boys in my peer group.

I joined the eighth-grade football team, where I was immediately placed on first string in the backfield. It was difficult to deny my capabilities, so I just went with it. Inwardly, I was still somewhat frail and lacking in confidence, but I learned to perform by willing myself to do so. After all, I had been blessed with a body that could respond better than most.

Things seemed to be looking up for me as I gained confidence in relation to my peers. I was making progress socially, and at home the fighting between my parents had seemed to subside. However, this was only the calm before the storm.

The next chapter of my life was one of extreme emotional turmoil, confusion, and pain. With puberty came the awakening of my sexual drive. Prior to this age I don't recall feeling sexually attracted to any individual, male or female. Even at this point, I wasn't sexually interested in anyone.

About this time my mother's youngest brother came to live with us. He was an exciting man and seemed to have everything going for him. He had nice clothes, drove nice cars, and apparently had his pick of beautiful women.

At this point I had no significant role model, so I took to him immediately. I started hanging around him and doing everything I could to be a part of whatever he would allow me to. I was fascinated with this older man whom I felt I could emulate. If I couldn't be like my father, maybe I could be like this guy.

After some time, he took an interest in me as well. This made me feel good. I had no significant preoccupation with him when he was not around, and I was not aware of any sexual attraction toward him. I was simply happy to be with him whenever time would permit.

One evening he asked me to give him a massage. I gladly obliged. Later that evening he molested me. I was about thirteen years old. This was the beginning of a three-year period of darkness and confusion that ultimately led me to my first thoughts of suicide. I still felt no significant sexual attractions. However, sex became the basis for how my uncle related to me for the next three years.

On my fifteenth birthday, my uncle took me out with him and some of his friends. He gave me large amounts of alcohol and marijuana. By the time he brought me home, it was two or three in the morning. As I stepped out of the car I couldn't feel the ground and fell flat on my face. He picked me up and carried me in through the back door so no one would see my state.

Later that evening I became violently ill due to excessive alcohol and marijuana. I experienced hot flashes, dizziness, vertigo (a spinning of the room), and vomiting. As I lay on the floor of my bedroom, I felt his presence on top of me. He tried to remove my undergarments. I said no and attempted to push him away. He physically restrained me and proceeded to rape me.

In the morning I awoke to find that he had cleaned up my vomit from the night before and all other signs of the incident. We never spoke a word about it. I erased all memories of the incident through denial and repression. I did not recall it again until I was over thirty years old.

My sex drive awakened sometime around fifteen years of age, in the midst of sexual molestation by my uncle. When I experienced sexual arousal for the first time, I felt guilty and ashamed. But he had an undeniable control over me. I did whatever he said. I felt as if I had no will to resist him.

Many of my friends were beginning to speak of relations with girls. I wanted to join them but felt as if I would be betraying my uncle. So I kept myself from situations in which I would encounter females in a sexual sort of way. This caused me extreme inner turmoil and heartache. I felt as if the world was passing me by.

I soon fell into a clinical depression. This would be the first of five episodes that I would experience throughout my journey to spiritual awakening. I became reclusive at home. I would come home from school, go into my bedroom, shut the door, and not come out until the next morning, then repeat the same cycle the next day. I have no idea how long this went on.

At age sixteen I obtained my driver's license. I started driving to meet my uncle for sexual rendezvous. I wanted to stop, but as was the story of my life up until this point, I had no strength of will to speak what I felt. I became disgusted with my uncle and hated myself for not being strong enough to refuse him.

One evening after basketball practice, the weight of this secret came crashing down on me. I could no longer hold up the image that I was emotionally well. I stood outside the locker room after practice, staring blankly out the window. A friend approached me and asked, "David, what's wrong?"

I turned to him with the intent of dismissing his inquiry with a vague response. When I saw the concern on his face, I broke down into a violent crying fit. He embraced me, trying to console my obvious distress. After I calmed down enough to speak, he released me. He asked directed questions, but I was mute. He invited me to his house that evening. I went, contemplating whether to tell him about my ordeal, but ultimately left without saying a word about it. We never spoke of it again.

I contacted this friend seventeen years later and revealed to him the mystery of that night after basketball practice. He still remembered.

Shortly after that night I began planning a way to commit suicide. I saw no other way out of my situation. I simply had no will to refuse my uncle. I wanted to get counseling but I knew my parents would need to be involved because I was underage. I could not burden my mother with this knowledge of her brother and me. My father had never been someone I could turn to with any emotional issue. Besides, I had rejected him years before and he was dead to me. There was no one else I trusted.

I found a razor blade and sat in my room with it aimed at my left wrist. I did not want to die but had no other idea of how to free myself from the life I lived. Then a thought came to my mind in the form of a small, quiet voice. *What about Me?* I immediately recognized the voice of God. I had forgotten my friend since I asked Him into my life eight years before. I thought, *Yes, He'll help me. He always has whenever I've asked Him to.* And so I began a journey to find Him.

I knew the God of the Bible. Though it had been years since I had spoken to Him, I felt sure I could find Him again if I searched hard enough. I found an old white Bible and began reading it after school each day, hoping to find something in its pages that would shed some light on my situation. I chose random passages by a method that was really none at all, and I did not understand much of what I read. Many mornings I would awaken to find the Book lying on my chest.

One night I was reading the gospel of John. I liked the part where Jesus said we could ask anything in His name and we would receive it (John 14:13—14).

When I got to the part about the crucifixion, I felt as if I were there, witnessing the event. When I read that Jesus said, "It is finished" (John 19:30), then He hung His head and died, I was shocked. I threw the Book down and wept uncontrollably. It was the first time I read this. "What is finished?" I cried. "I thought You said I could ask anything of You. How can I ask You to free myself from this life of misery if You couldn't even free Yourself?"

I threw myself on the bed and sobbed quietly. I contemplated the possibility that God might be a figment of my imagination. If this were the case, my searching was useless and there was no hope for me. I really was all alone in the world.

I mustered the faith to pray one last prayer. "God, I'm not sure if You exist, but if You can hear me, how long will it be before You help me?"

An amazing thing happened. I heard the sound of rushing waters flowing powerfully around the room. My eyes blurred. I'm not sure if that was due to my tears or if the atmosphere of the room had actually changed.

Then a presence descended into the room, similar to the wave of heat that had healed my stomach ache years ago. My body trembled, and immediately I felt peace. I could not see God, but I felt His presence all around me. I said, "Lord, it's You. You're here!"

I lay there, basking in this amazing presence and peace. I had no worries. I knew He was with me and that all would be okay. How could it not be? I felt loved beyond anything I had ever experienced. The God of the whole universe had heard me and chosen to visit me in my time of distress. My Friend was here once again.

I heard a small, still voice say, "Follow me." I turned to my right because I was certain someone had spoken the words aloud. But no one was visibly there.

After He spoke, the room went back to normal. There was no more blurred vision and no more sound of rushing waters, simply stillness and silence. But I was filled with hope and joy. God had actually visited me. I wanted to tell my mother, so I jumped from my bed, ran to the door, and opened it. I found her in the living room, sitting on my father's lap, watching television. My emotions were a mess, so I steadied myself to call for her.

I did not want my dad to know I had been crying. I didn't want to be even more of a disappointment to him. So I whispered, "Ma?"

They both looked up.

"What is wrong with you?" she asked.

"Just come here."

She came into my bedroom and I began weeping. I told her what had just happened and how God had visited me. I did not tell her of my struggles. She prayed with me and I went to sleep.

The next day I awakened with a sense of newness in my life. I no longer felt down. The depression had lifted and I felt free. It was as if I'd been reborn, a new person.

Sometime later, my uncle called for me. I went to his apartment, not like before but with a certainty of mind. He sensed something different in me. He tried to touch me and I withdrew. I was distant and cold toward him.

I felt empowered. My will had become strengthened. I no longer wanted this abnormal relationship and felt the courage to communicate that. After all, I was sixteen and more than physically capable of controlling my immediate environment. Unlike before, I now saw myself as capable.

He looked at me, bewildered, and said, "You don't want this anymore, do you?"

"No, I don't," I replied. Without any further discussion, I left him in that apartment. I didn't even look back.

The next time I spoke to him was in my sophomore year in college, three years later. It was a brief interaction.

The last time I spoke to him was at age twenty-nine. I was in my second year of medical residency training. My mother told me he was ill in a hospital approximately two hours away. I went to visit him, but he never saw me due to large amounts of sedation. His doctors were perplexed as to the severity of illness in such a young, previously healthy man. I told them his history and insisted they perform an HIV test. Shortly after my visit, he died due to complications of HIV-related pneumonia.

The stand I took with my uncle in the apartment was a new beginning for me. Now free from his grip, I felt the need to begin living life as a normal young man. This included dating and socializing. I was excited about my new start, but was soon halted by personal struggle and disappointment. The years of sexual abuse by my uncle had taken an undeniable toll on my psyche. Though outwardly normal, emotionally I was a wreck.

Up until this point, I had not told anyone of my ordeal with my uncle, though I suspect it did not go unnoticed by my siblings or my parents. Our family lived in denial about many things. This was no exception.

I tried dating but was too emotionally unstable to experience normal relating with a female. I recall sitting in a car with one of my first girlfriends. We were talking when a song began playing on the radio. It took me back to a time when I was under the spell of my uncle. I tried to shut off the radio, but I lost control of my emotions in a crying fit. My girlfriend was shocked.

I bid her good-bye and drove away. The relationship ended soon after. To this day I cannot recall her name.

My next failed attempt at dating was enough to squelch any future attempts at relations with females for the next two years. A friend of mine had been interested in me for over a year. She was nice and I liked her. However, I'd always had some excuse as to why I would not go out with her, for this was during the time when my uncle's influence was at its height. Now that I was free I decided to approach her from a romantic perspective.

We were at a friend's house and his parents were not home. She and I ended up in a bedroom. As things progressed toward a sexual encounter, she said she wanted to stop. She made it clear that she was not ready for a sexual encounter.

Like any young man, I tried to talk her into it. My focus was not really on her at the time. It was completely selfish. I felt I had to prove to myself that I was not gay.

She reluctantly acquiesced. But I was too preoccupied with performance to actually perform. The act was more of a task for me. It had nothing to do with the normal affection and subsequent sexual arousal experienced between two individuals mutually connected in an emotional bond.

When she realized that I was stricken with a severe case of impotence, she laughed, I think more out of relief than cruelty. She actually felt sad for me. She smiled and insisted that we try again some other time.

Devastated, I drove home screaming at the top of my lungs. I asked God, "Why did you make me this way? I must be gay." Not only did I not feel a normal physical attraction for females, but I'd started to notice a distinct sexual interest in certain individuals of the same sex. Now, in full-blown adolescence, the sex drive was alive and powerful. I hated myself for the feelings that had emerged. But I could do nothing to stop them.

My plan was to try ignoring them. Their intensity was such that I didn't even consider that they could be tamed. I would stop dating females and simply ignore my interest in certain male peers. In retrospect, this was not a good idea. It only created an internal pressure cooker that erupted years later.

I graduated from high school and moved away to college. I thought that leaving my hometown would bring with it a new lease on life. But no matter where I went, I always brought myself with me. I fared well academically. But internally, I remained in torment.

I joined Bible studies. I was active in dorm life and athletics. I even developed a core group of male Christian friends whom I felt very little attraction for. Regardless of my achievements at suppressing and ignoring my abnormal drives, I wrestled with masturbation, of which male imagery was the primary focus. This was something my uncle had taught me years before.

I recall walking back to my dorm room from classes, crying and pleading with God to remove the images from my mind. I was plagued with memories and images of the past that I'd been freed from years earlier. No matter how hard I tried to ignore them, I felt as if they were being forced into my mind by an unknown power. I had no strength to block them. It was like living in constant torture.

I made countless pleas to God. I promised Him that if He would remove this torment in my mind, I would serve Him all the days of my life. Looking back on this prayer from my current vantage point of maturity, I realize I had not yet learned that God does not free us so that we will serve Him. Out of obedience, we serve Him until He frees us.

How I managed to focus on my studies is beyond my grasp. My masculine spiritual makeup served me well, for duty and task are strengths of the masculine mind.

One morning about eight o'clock, I was in my dorm room, studying for an exam I had to take in the next few hours. A friend of mine entered the room dressed only in his underwear. We spoke for a moment and then he left. This was not an uncommon experience. However, the incident ignited a fury of images that came pouring down on me like an avalanche. My heart started racing, I began sweating, and all the muscles in my body tightened at once.

The most intense feelings of sexual arousal that I'd ever experienced overshadowed me. I felt afraid, as if my body had been taken over by some unknown force. Myriad sexual images flooded my mind. For a few seconds I resisted this attack with all that was in my will. Finally, when I felt that I would die from its intensity, I slammed my head on my desk and yelled, "Jesus, help me, please!"

Immediately after I cried out to God, the oppression lifted as if it had never happened. In an instant, my heart stopped pounding. The sweating ceased, the muscle tension dissipated, and the extreme sexual excitement vanished.

I lifted my head and looked about the room. There was complete silence and an eerie stillness. I felt as if my assailant had been vanquished. My God had once again come to my aid. However, I became aware of another presence that was bent on securing my undoing, for this was clearly not a normal incident. The rapidness by which it entered was only matched by the speed in which it lifted from me. I had come under spiritual attack.

This was the first time I became aware of a spiritual dimension to my struggles. It frightened me. I grabbed my things and left my dorm room. I told no one of the incident.

Later that year I returned home for a rare visit with my family. We all went to my aunt's house for the holidays, as was common for our family at the time. As usual, the adults sat around the dining room table telling stories, trading insights, and sharing wisdom with one another. We called this "the table of the elders." No children sat there. We kids played in some other area of the house. But at times we came to the table and listened to the wisdom of the elders.

When I came home from college that day, I sat at the adult table, feeling as if I had come of age and could offer something of value. The conversation moved toward my experiences as a young man. As I spoke, my aunt apparently perceived an emotional instability in me. My mother and father sensed an angry undercurrent. The room became quiet.

"David," my aunt asked, "do you still hurt about some of the things of your past?"

"No," I answered quickly. I denied any insinuation that I was unhappy in any regard. After all, I was home from college and had earned the right to sit at this table. But immediately following this response, I was overcome by such an extreme emotional pain that I digressed into a violent crying fit.

My mother and father ran to me in an attempt to console my distress, but there was nothing that could be done or said. My pain was deeper than I could have imagined. I was once again undone. I felt confused as to how unstable my emotions were, even years after my escape from home.

As my parents drove me home that night, I lay in the backseat while they sat in the front. They argued with each other. I don't recall what they argued about. I felt numb, tired, and emotionally drained. I cared nothing about the fight that ensued just feet in front of me. It was a scene all too familiar to me.

That incident taught me to avoid all discussions regarding my father, home life, and childhood.

One night I was in my dorm room with my Christian college buddies when we began a discussion about our fathers. As I began giving my input, I felt overcome with unspeakable grief. This preceded a crying fit that lasted about two minutes. My friends were as shocked as I was. No one said anything, but after I regained control, I simply apologized and we moved the conversation to another topic. No one spoke further of the incident.

I decided after that to avoid all discussions of my family life in public situations. I was still in denial as to the severity of my emotional wounds, so I did not consider seeking professional help.

I became increasingly dependent on my college friends. We were practically inseparable. Centered around our faith, we had a camaraderie I cherished.

My junior year was right around the corner and I sensed an inclination to apply for a job as a resident assistant. It came with the added benefit of free room and board.

I figured my friends would move with me. However, most of them felt a desire to move out of the dorm. Freedom from authority is the ultimate step toward independent living.

I was saddened to hear that I was the only one who would be staying in the dorms the following year. This brought with it memories of loneliness from a past I thought I had escaped. I began the familiar retreat into seclusion.

My friends wondered what the problem was, but we rarely spoke candidly about awkward situations. I knew my odd behavior was noticeable. However, I had no idea how to just be normal and let things fall as they may.

My attachment to these friends was never based on sexual feelings, just genuine friendship. However, my need for these guys showed a lack of personal independence in my own right. Looking back, I now see how this degree of emotional dependence, even among platonic friends, is unhealthy. I understand now why God chose to separate me from them.

I knew I had to do something to stop the awkwardness I was bringing to the group. I chose a secluded place in the basement of our dorm building to seek an encounter with my God. In tears I told Him of my fears and insecurities. I told Him about my fear of loneliness and abandonment. I asked Him, "Why would You give me such good friends only to snatch them from me just when I was beginning to feel comfortable?"

I sat there in silence for a long moment. Then I fell into a trance-like state and found myself in a kind of vision. I was no longer in the basement of my dormitory. I was suspended in a black void. I was holding on to a very thin string suspended in nothingness. There was a tiny light above me. It shone on the string just enough to reveal its structure. It appeared to be no more substantial than the thread of a spider web.

How could this web hold me? I felt as if it would snap at any moment, so I looked down to see where I would land. Beneath me I saw nothingness, an endless, deep, black pit. At this discovery I began to panic, saying over and over, "I'm going to fall. I'm going to fall."

I then heard the still, small voice that had become so familiar to me. "Look down again." I looked down. To my surprise there was now a large right hand spread out beneath me. I marveled as I contemplated this sight. Then the small and peaceful voice of my friend came again. "If you fall, I'll catch you."

I immediately snapped out of the vision and was once again in the basement of my dormitory building. I knew what God meant by this vision. He wanted to communicate to me that no matter how unstable and unsure I felt my situation was, He would be there to catch me. I needed to trust in Him completely, forsaking all others, including friendships that He had blessed me with for a season.

With this lesson, I was once again at peace. God had promised to catch me if I fell. My faith in this was all that I needed to be free of the fear that I would once again be alone.

I left that basement released from the anxiety of loneliness and returned to a normal, friendly relationship with my buddies. Later God took me to the Bible verse that says, "So do not fear, for I am with you; do not be dismayed, for I am your God. I will strengthen you and help you; I will uphold you with my righteous right hand" (Isaiah 41:10).

At about twenty years of age, I decided I would become a physician. I was inspired in this direction by my mother. Life was hard for her, but against all odds she'd obtained a college education. I respected her drive to persevere through her formidable circumstances. She was my earthly anchor when things got rough.

When I was a sophomore in college, I revealed to my parents the secret of my abuse. I sat at the dining room table, cried, and told them of about my struggles. They responded in shock and disbelief. Tears were shed and some token advice given. I do not recall what.

I then told my mother and father about my uncle's treachery. They did not know how to handle this information. Though I was an emotional wreck, I think they took some solace in the fact that I had begun developing a mild attraction to females. I think they assumed that I was only going through a phase and that I was really just fine.

This was another way in which I feel my parents lived in denial about my emotional state. They offered no recommendations for counseling. They never spoke to me about it again. It became the elephant in the room whenever signs of my struggles would become clear to them. There was never any concrete engagement with me regarding the subject.

Eventually, it became common knowledge in my family that some form of abuse had taken place between my uncle and me. Even my brothers and sisters knew. No one ever brought it up directly, but I could tell they'd heard by certain comments they made. It was a family secret that no one wanted to acknowledge.

No matter what my family members say, I'm certain my abuse did not go completely unnoticed at the time it occurred. My family lived in denial about many facets of our existence. I'm sure this was related to the denial and dysfunction my siblings and I observed in our parents' relationship. We'd learned to assume that life was the way it was. Just accept it. Don't even try to expect any better.

Following my mother's example, most of my siblings, like me, excelled academically and career-wise. However, marriage and interpersonal relating was the Achilles heel of my families' relationships. This is a testament to the denial we all learned to live with. No one ever sought help for anything.

Our parents often told us, "Children should be seen and not heard." I don't believe they meant harm by this. They simply wanted us to be quiet. But it gave us the impression that our opinions and thoughts didn't matter.

After I told my parents of the abuse that evening, I felt a sense of release but still had no idea how to navigate interpersonally. I had spilled the beans about my uncle, my most terrible secret. But I felt as if I had not said a word to anyone.

By my senior year in college, I began to notice a dramatic sexual interest in certain females. This was exciting for me, but I felt little confidence relating to women. I was still haunted by the incident in high school where I was embarrassed due to my inability to perform sexually. Furthermore, the homosexual attractions had not diminished in the least. With the beginnings of this new interest in females, I became internally conflicted.

My parents tried to set me up with a certain female friend of the family. I think this was their attempt to confirm that I was really okay. Eventually, I began dating this woman and we had some great times together. I really liked her, but I could not tell her about my personal struggles. I was too ashamed. I felt unfit. I could not risk humiliation again. So I played along, taking solace in the fact that sexual relating should be reserved for marriage. The subject was never brought up between us. After all, we were both Christians.

Just prior to my twenty-first birthday, I was nearing the end of my undergraduate career. This is a time of anxiety for most college students. It is a time when you face the reality of adulthood, for college is only an extension of high school in one form or another. The difficulties of holding down a steady job, paying bills, and family rearing are all foreign concepts to the graduating senior. Most are not ready for it, and I was no exception. I still had not progressed past puberty in my ability to relate in a normal way to the opposite sex.

The promise of medical school offered me another four years of freedom from the real world. So I readied myself to master the MCAT and began preparing for admission to medical school. These became my primary goals. I had no idea what to do about my emotional situation.

As I neared the end of my senior year, another bout with depression came crashing in like a flood. I felt lost, like a ship drifting without a sail. My future was uncertain. Outwardly, I appeared put together, but internally was another story.

I had not spoken to God for approximately one year. Though He had shown Himself to be a reality to me, I could not understand why He offered me nothing in regard to my sexual struggles. I began to accept the idea that I was homosexual and there was nothing I or God could do about it.

The decision to believe this lie marked the beginning of a ten-year battle that cost me nearly everything in the end. I withdrew socially. I confined myself to my room for days. I began losing weight from not eating.

I broke up with my girlfriend. I no longer wanted to play along. I wanted to feel normal, even if that meant going down the path to homosexuality.

I started visiting a female strip club. I sat there for hours, watching these women. I liked the way they made me feel. I was definitely attracted to them. But it was easier to admire them from afar than to risk personal contact with one.

On one occasion, a woman in the audience approached me. She sat down and we began to talk. I was naïve at this point but it quickly became clear what her intentions were. I hesitated, afraid and unsure of myself. But the depressed state of mind I was in assured me that I would eventually lose all inhibitions in this situation.

I took her back to my dorm room, and just prior to my twenty-first birthday, I lost my virginity. Surprisingly, there was nothing wrong with me sexually. Physically, I performed and felt normal with her. It was a most pleasurable experience. She had no idea of my internal pain. She spent the night, and later that morning we spoke casually and she offered me her phone number. I gladly took it. She kissed me, said good-bye, and left. I never spoke to her again. But I remember her name to this day.

This experience with the woman at the bar was the beginning of a slippery slope. Armed with the knowledge that I could function normally with females, I began dating a woman on campus. She was fun and vibrant. Our relationship quickly progressed to a sexual one that lasted through the remainder of the school year. It ended when I moved away later that summer.

However, I continued to be haunted by homosexual attractions. I could not understand this. How could I be sexually satisfied with females and yet have these worrisome attractions to certain men? With my inhibitions long since abandoned, I decided to try my hand at a homosexual experience. I wanted to see if it was all in my head.

I answered an ad in the campus newsletter from another student seeking this sort of interaction. I don't recall anything sexual on our first meeting. I was too uncertain about an actual encounter with a man. In my mind it seemed appropriate, but with him present I felt awkward.

On a subsequent meeting, I decided to just go with the flow. This eventually ended in my first willful homosexual experience as an adult. It was nothing like I thought it would be, not nearly as pleasing as my female conquests.

After he left I became ill. Though he was long gone, I could still smell his scent all over me. Nauseated and on the verge of vomiting, I rushed into the shower and tried to scrub any trace of his scent from my body.

I began crying. I hated what I had become. Not only had I violated God's law with women, but now also with a man. I attempted to call out to my Friend, but my guilt blocked any faith that He would hear me.

Eventually, I stopped all attempts at communication with Him. The disappointment I was sure He felt toward me must have been unthinkable. Like the day my dad found me hiding on the bench during a football game, I believed God had looked at me and, in disgust, turned away without a word.

For the next five years God was like a ghostly presence that I knew was ever present, but I did not speak to Him anymore.

The guilt, physical nausea, and disappointing sexual experience with this male student was not enough to keep me from future experimentations with men. Looking back, I can see the compulsory nature of the homosexual attractions. One would have thought that negative sexual encounter would have convinced me that homosexuality was not for me. But I still felt drawn to it. The worrisome images in my mind persisted as powerful as ever. They were much more enticing than the physical encounters. I did not understand this. But those powerful mental images drove me toward another male contact.

I visited some gay bars. Eventually, the male encounters became less distressing. But I could not shake the sense of disgust that I felt in the gay bar scene. Furthermore, I began to notice that I was more interested in physical closeness with men than a sexual transaction of any kind. But sexual interactions are what the gay scene is all about.

I eventually decided that I was not interested in what this life had to offer. I was aroused by the physical images of masculinity, but there was always an extreme focus on physical sexual contact, something I was not inclined to be a part of. The idea of sexual contact with a man was more desirable than actually experiencing it.

After about two years I bade farewell to the gay bar scene. All the while, I continued to have girlfriends and enjoyed sexual relations without much difficulty. I came to the conclusion that I was bent toward women, but the homosexual problem continued to plague me. It became extremely confusing at times. Sex with women was different from sexual contact with men. With women came a sense of comfort that I never experienced with a man. However, men offered something powerfully enticing that I could not find in a woman. I was torn, so I decided I would have both.

During this time, at approximately twenty-one years of age, I met the woman who would become my wife several years later. She was nice, beautiful, and alluring. I was intrigued by her beauty.

We began dating. But I soon realized that she was interested in far more than I was able to offer. She had a three-year-old daughter and did not want to waste time in the dating scene. She needed the security of a family life for her and her little girl. I did not feel up to the task.

Our courtship lasted approximately one year. I was then hit with my third bout of clinical depression. For the first time I sought professional help. I went to one session, quickly decided that the counselor could not help me, and never returned.

For the next four years I drifted. I had a few girlfriends, and on rare occasions I made contact with a man. This was usually during times of extreme stress, for I was in the midst of medical school training at the time.

I soon decided that I could no longer tolerate random sexual contact with men. It seemed dirty, made me feel unhappy, and filled me with a sense of self-loathing beyond comprehension. I wanted their closeness in an emotional sense, but not their physical advances. I made the decision to abandon all forms of sexual contact with random men. I was already unhappy and saw no need to compound the situation with this behavior.

With the exception of an infrequent occurrence, my experimenting was over. I was approximately twenty-three years of age.

Still plagued by homosexual temptation in the form of mental imagery, I finally discovered a gold mine that turned out to be my nemesis for the next eight years and even followed me even into my marriage years later.

This discovery was the Internet. It was discreet and offered me the visual images of men without the complication of physically being with them. This habit quickly turned into an addiction.

I was now free to be with women physically while entertaining pornographic images in private. It seemed the best of both worlds … until I discovered a loose end. I was still not immune to homosexual contact under the right circumstances.

On occasion I experienced physical attraction toward a male friend. I took the utmost care not to reveal these feelings. I soon noticed a pattern. I discovered that new male acquaintances bothered me very little, if at all, in regard to physical attraction. But occasionally, I found myself attracted to an individual I had become close with in a friendly sort of a way.

I was not interested in sexual contact with men for the sake of sex. I wanted an emotional bond with them. But my sexual drive was somehow connected to my emotional drive. I became sexually interested only in men I felt close to emotionally. It stood to reason that my sexual attractions were not the primary driving force. My emotional problem secondarily drove my sexuality. This explained my lack of interest in the gay bar scene. It was all about sex, without an emotional tie.

The male images that had plagued me since I left my uncle standing in the apartment were a result of the molestation that occurred in the dawn of my awakening sexuality. I connected sexual arousal with men because it was with a man that I experienced my first sexual excitement in puberty. The three-year period of abuse solidified the behavior in my mind through repetition.

Those images were a remnant of the abuse suffered at the hands of my uncle. Pornographic male imagery connected me to the beginnings of my sexual awakening. Without a personality associated with them, they were powerful. They lacked the complicated status of sex with men with whom I had no emotional connection. They were only pictures. I could not touch them and they could not touch me.

It was now clear that I had an emotional problem and it was complicating my sexual functioning. But understanding this did not offer me any answers on how to fix it. So I figured that was just the way it was. This acceptance ultimately led me into my first homosexual relationship.

I decided that I would not involve myself with random men, but if a personal acquaintance became available, I could have the best of both worlds: physical contact with a man I felt close to emotionally.

That situation presented itself later in my medical school training, not with a classmate but with an outside acquaintance. I made sure to keep my professional life separate from my emotional life. But to my dismay, this short-lived relationship was plagued by the difficulties associated with all male-male intimate relating: jealousies, violence, issues of control and dominance, promiscuity, and lack of fidelity. This connection quickly became filled with turmoil.

With this relationship came my fourth bout with clinical depression. Suicide again became a viable option. I began losing weight and stopped eating. After about eight months, I decided I no longer wanted the relationship to be physical. With all the promise of sexual contact with an emotional connection, I still did not feel right about it. Instead of finding freedom in the relationship, it seemed I had become a prisoner to it. My sexual attraction for this friend disappeared. I knew I would have to end our relationship.

I withdrew into seclusion, but my friend pursued me in hopes of pulling me back in. In light of the emotional bond I had with him, it was not as easy to dismiss him as I did the gay bar scene. Those individuals were not my friends.

In desperation I once again called on God. I had not spoken to Him for approximately five years. I had gotten myself in a jam and I could not will myself free. He was my only hope.

I also decided to call my mother and tell her about my situation. She and my sisters began a prayer vigil for me.

My friend was aware of my desire to be free from the relationship but took solace in the fact that my will was weak. One night, as I sat in the living room of his home, I fell into a kind of trance. It was similar to the one I had when God stretched out His hand beneath me during my sophomore year in college. During this vision, I apparently continued communicating with the people in the room because they didn't notice that anything had changed for me.

I was sitting on a high mountaintop. The sun was bright and there were beautiful clouds in the sky. The day was perfect and peaceful. I stood at the edge of the mountain on its far end, where it dropped off steeply at a cliff. The fall would be great. I could not even see the ground beneath. I stepped closer. I hesitated, and then a flurry of words became audible in my left ear. "Jump! Jump! Jump! Let go. Jump!" The words were violent and forceful, doing everything but pushing me off that cliff.

As I leaned forward to jump, I became aware of a presence to my right. It was pleasant but firm, and it spoke not a word. But it communicated its wishes to my mind: "No, don't do it."

For a second I wavered in the valley of indecision. Jumping would put an end to my struggle. But I would be actively leaving the presence on my right once and for all. It seemed to care for me in a way that the voice on my left did not. I started to feel as if the left voice hated me. The flurry of its words continued, loud and angrily, while on my right, the still presence spoke not a word.

I took a deep breath, sighed, and sat down. Then I said, "I cannot jump." With those words I was back in the living room of my friend's home. I looked around and perceived that no one had noticed my departure.

I knew what the vision meant. The cliff represented the mountain of homosexuality. The sun, clouds, and beauty of the day represented the promise of fulfillment. The jump represented my decision to accept it once and for all. The voice on my left was Satan and the presence on my right was God. My Friend was still with me after all these years.

"God," I prayed, "I don't know how I got here, but please help me. I want to come home."

I knew at that moment that I would leave my male friend. I just needed to figure out how, for he was extremely disturbed emotionally. It was in this relationship that I, for the first time, realized the emotional sickness of homosexuality in someone other than myself. He was violent and docile in a cyclical fashion. He was controlling, violent, and prone to fits of rage, but in the next second became an innocent, whimpering child full of neediness and wanting comfort. I was bewildered and perplexed at how quickly his moods changed. It was as if he had a "Jekyll and Hyde" personality. It was a fearful thing to behold.

I remember trying to come up with a psychiatric diagnosis to explain his behaviors. The closest I got was borderline personality disorder. But still this didn't come close to explaining his behaviors.

I tried to free myself from this person. He was unstable beyond belief. There were times when I had to literally fight him. At this point I cared nothing for what it would take. If getting free meant a physical fight, then so be it. My mind was fixed. I did not want this relationship anymore, at least not in the way it had developed.

I prayed and sought God daily. My conversations became full of focus on God and His love for me. This talk infuriated my friend. On one occasion, he slammed the door to my car so violently the inner panel was torn loose. He knew this kind of talk would mean the end of the relationship. And he was bent on saving it at all costs.

On another occasion, I witnessed and unbelievable event. To this day I have not experienced a display of spiritual manifestation to this degree. I was speaking of Jesus to my friend when he screamed in a voice full of hate, malice, and anger, "Jesus is dead!"

I was terrified. I had clearly been addressed by a demonic spirit of some sort. I mustered the courage to respond, "No, He's not dead. He is alive."

My friend screamed, got up, and ran from my apartment, slamming the door violently. Later on, he said to me, "David, I give up. You win. I can't fight your God. He is too strong for me." He soon stopped coming around.

I made up my mind to leave homosexuality once and for all. But I had no idea what to do about my mental struggles. I was still addicted to Internet pornography. Furthermore, I had not yet tackled the roots of my emotional disturbance.

God understood that my sexual attractions were not really the issue. They were being driven by secondary issues revolving around my painful childhood experiences and a rift in my relationship with my father. God did not want me to just be free from the outward manifestations of my pain. He wanted me to tackle the source. When God heals, He heals completely, not in part.

I was still inextricably focused on my attractions. But I continued to live in denial of my past. I would at some point have to face my past and learn to forgive it. My journey to healing was not yet complete.

As He did when I was sixteen, God had rescued me from a sudden-death sort of experience. I sought counseling at a local church. But as is common in the Christian church today, I found little in the form of support for my problem.

I told my family that I had left the unhealthy relationship, and once again they were silent. We rarely spoke about it. I was alone again with this monkey on my back.

God had once again rescued me through empowering my will. But He remained silent as to the possibility of emotional healing for me. I decided there was none. The best I could do was try to contain it. But I would not become an open homosexual.

Though He offered me no explanation or plan of escape, my God was clearly against this. Though He slayed me, yet would I trust Him (Job 13:15).

I knew I would not jump. Satan had offered me that option and I had refused it. I was nearing the end of my medical training and decided that I would settle down. Of all my female companions, and there were many to choose from, one woman came to mind: Varee. Though we were not an item, over the years she continued to contact me periodically for friendly conversation, or an occasional card would show up in the mail. This was no easy task because I moved yearly.

This display of fidelity intrigued me. I wondered what it was she liked in me that produced this degree of commitment. I knew she would stick by me no matter what. I needed a friend like that. So after many years, I gave her a call. I did not know what her personal situation was at the time.

I told her I had been through some rough times since we last spoke and I was in no way ready to be anything more than just her friend. She gladly accepted my invitation to talk on a regular basis. As time went forward, our talks increased and my depression began to lift.

Eventually, I was well enough to begin socializing with my friends again. Prior to my escape from the relationship with my friend, there was a year or more when I was lost to everyone, family and friends. I started going out to the clubs (not gay) with my buddies like old times. I felt a sense of freedom. Though I was still addicted to Internet pornography, I had no desire for physical contact with any men.

One night at the club, I met a woman. She was pretty, and I was attracted to her. We talked, and at the end of the evening she gave me her phone number. I was feeling back to normal and I enjoyed the freedom from involvement in the gay world.

The next weekend I grabbed her number and picked up the phone. No sooner than I did this I heard God ask, "What about Varee?" As I sat there with the phone in my hand, I saw another vision. Above me were pictures of two women. The one on the left was the woman I was about to call and the one on the right was Varee. I sat there perplexed. Again He said, "Choose, Son. You cannot have both."

I felt the correction of a loving father who had strongly set boundaries for his son. This foolishness of womanizing and non-commitment had to stop. I hung my head, looked again at the images, and said to God, "Okay, then. I choose her." I pointed to Varee. I then tore up the other woman's number and threw it away. I never called her.

If I was no longer open to having a committed homosexual relationship, and I was not allowed to have free reign with women, I had only two options: celibacy or a wife. The choice was an easy one. I made up my mind that I would marry Varee if she would have me.

I intensified my pursuit of her. I even called my dad to discuss it with him. He had long since left his old ways. He'd found God and was now a pastor of a small church. This was a hard thing for me to accept because I could only see who he used to be. I did not know my dad as a pastor. Nevertheless, I wanted his approval. I wanted him to be proud of me and I knew this decision would make him happy. We did not speak of my past struggles. He simply advised me to marry her.

I bought a ring and proposed to her the next week. She said yes. As she pondered our future together, God spoke to her concerning her decision to accept me as her husband. As she sat on her bed one evening in meditation, He said to her, "Go. I will be with you." With that, she rested.

We had the makings of a great friendship. However, I was bothered by the fact that she knew nothing of my past and current struggles with Internet pornography. This loophole would ultimately end in my slip into another homosexual relationship. Secrets of this sort between spouses is the foothold Satan needs to poison the pot.

My next battle with the mountain of homosexuality would be the greatest. It brought with it the most severe form of depression I had experienced up until this point and lasted for approximately one and a half years. The intensity of this depressive episode was gut wrenching. And if that was not enough, the length of time that it stayed with me was seemingly unbearable. It was in this state that I came the closest to committing suicide.

I met a gentlemen named Adam at my athletic facility and noticed a familiar attraction. It had been over a year and a half since I left the previous homosexual relationship. I was in the midst of my medical internship, tired and fatigued. The hours I worked were unbelievable. The combination of fatigue and the residual habit of masturbation and pornography got the best of me.

It became clear that there was a mutual interest in an intimate relationship. This was even more distressing because I was now engaged to be married.

Weak willed and full of fear, I tried to ignore the coming catastrophe. Eventually, I told my new friend about my engagement, but I did not tell my wife about him. I knew it would come to a head at some point, but in the meantime, I used denial for all it was worth. I had not told my wife about my past and now it had become a part of our relationship without her knowledge. I loved my fiancée but had no idea how to drop this bombshell. Though I believed in her fidelity to me, I had no idea how she would respond to this information. I was so outwardly put together it did not fit her image of me. I didn't have the humility to show her my true brokenness. If I did, I'd risk her leaving me, and the fear of loneliness was stifling.

I decided that I would just live in the moment. This worked as long as my two worlds did not collide. But on my wedding day, the inner angst was unbearable. I had asked my dad to perform our ceremony. I knew he would be proud to do this. I wanted him to be proud of me.

In my heart, I resented him for not probing me and forcing out my secret. I felt that he did not care about my obvious emotional distress. My parents were clearly aware of my struggles. I did not understand why they had never asked me if I was truly ready for the commitment I was about to make. Maybe they thought I was fine. I don't know. We never talked about it. The show would go on, but I was alone once again.

Prior to the ceremony, I sat in the front room with my father and my best man, my brother. All was silent. I was clearly nervous and anxious. I think they blew it off as wedding-day jitters. My loneliness was extreme even with my father and brother at my side. I needed rescuing. I wanted to tell my secret, but to whom?

I heard the music start playing and began to feel emotionally unstable. I immediately recognized a familiar presence in the place. It was the same presence I felt when God visited me twelve years ago in my bedroom as a sixteen-year-old boy. I had not seriously spoken to God for some time. My guilt was too extreme and would not allow me to approach Him.

I marveled at His visit on this day. Why would He come to me at a time when I was in violation of all that was pure and holy? I was about to marry a woman who knew nothing of my terrible secret.

This is the love of God. At my most critical hour, He saw my need, not my sin. I was terrified, scared, alone, and in need of a father's comforting word. He had been silently watching me even in my rebellion toward Him. Not saying anything, yet remaining close, as a mother quietly hovers close by while her child wanders in a nearby field. The child does not see her but she is there. Her eyes are ever watchful and ready to react at the first sign of danger.

God knew everything about me, yet He still came to me at this moment when I needed His strength. Like the commitment displayed by Varee years before, here He was, faithful to me. He would not leave me alone.

I turned my head toward the wall and gritted my teeth. I felt that God must love me beyond comprehension. He spoke no words and I saw no visions. I just felt His presence holding and comforting me. I expected Him to tell me to stop, given the secret I held. But He said nothing, and I felt that this was His will for my life. That gave me the courage to continue.

I loved Varee but had no idea how I could be the husband she expected and deserved. I took solace in the fact that God stood by my side. Though He gave no answer I knew that somehow all would be well one day with Varee and me.

I began to quietly sob. My father and brother watched me. No words were spoken. The ceremony went forth as planned.

I thought on many occasions about how I could end the relationship with Adam, but he had become a confidant. He was the only one who knew of my plight and seemed to accept me without question. He became my trusted companion. This made our connection even stronger.

At times our relationship was platonic, but sexual encounters soon became the norm. I tried to maintain a facade that all was well, but I was sure my wife sensed that something was not right with me. I was never intentionally cruel to her. But I was emotionally absent. I spent hours working and taking extra jobs that we did not need, anything to take my mind off the lie I had created. Financially, we were well off, for I was now a practicing physician. The extra money meant nothing. And God was once again silent.

After my first daughter was born I noticed a strange irritation with Adam. He resented the fact that he was a big secret in my life. This created a strain in the relationship. In the end, he really had no reason to stick around. I felt the relationship becoming unstable. I could have let it end. But I had grown accustomed to my male companion. And I had been in such staunch denial about my life for so many years, my spiritual eyesight was gone. I was in utter darkness.

God had long since vanished from my thoughts. I was a robot, mechanical and adept at juggling lies. My heart had become numb. I could no longer distinguish between what was truth and what was a lie. My work increased, and in my free time I fell further into Internet pornography.

Adam's resentment of my family life was becoming all too apparent, though we rarely spoke about the issue. But I would not leave home for him. He started to feel that our relationship was a dead end. I now had a wife, a stepdaughter, and a baby girl. The stakes were too high. I certainly couldn't leave at this stage in the game.

I felt that I needed his male companionship. But with the relationship becoming unpredictable, replacing him seemed like the best option.

Soon another man came into my life who was in a similar situation to mine. Steve was married with a couple of children but struggling with his sexuality. He had no desire to leave his family, so he seemed a better match for me than Adam, who was single.

I thought that replacing Adam would be rather uneventful, but it turned out that our bond was not easily broken. Adam was still in my life, so he and Steve sometimes overlapped, even though neither one was aware of the situation, and neither was my wife. My problem now involved multiple people, children, wives, and families.

I couldn't juggle such a mess. Satan had me and he knew it. It was only a matter of time before I began to crack.

Another bout of depression took hold of me. One day I was sitting in my car outside my house. I didn't want to go inside. The truth about my life began breaking through the wall of denial I had used to shield me from the reality of my situation. I felt as if my mind had started to bend as this Matrix began to fall. The weight of my deception pressed hard on me. I felt a heaviness on my head.

Images of my wife, my children, Adam, Steve, and Steve's family all whirled around in my mind. My vision blurred and I slumped against the steering wheel. I felt as if I were on the verge of physical death. This attack was similar to the one I had in my dorm room years earlier. I felt powerless. I was no longer worthy to call on God. I had long since lost sight of Him.

I figured this was the end for me and I accepted it. Then, in a fraction of a second, the heaviness lifted. I knew I would not die that day, but I was still terrified. I realized that I was again under spiritual attack, but now I had no God to call on. I felt truly lost.

With the falling of my Matrix, I had difficulty looking at Varee. I lost practically all capability to perform sexually with her. I started sleeping on the sofa. Conversations with her ended. My inward spiral had begun.

Varee finally told me that she felt we were living different lives under the same roof. I simply looked at her and then turned away without a word. Steve had been having similar problems. I knew the time of exposure was imminent. Actually, I welcomed it. I felt like an animal lying in the street, half alive and half dead. I just wanted it to be over. It was time to pay the piper.

Steve's wife contacted my wife and the suspense ended. Varee would have to begin her own painful journey to personal healing. Our entire existence together was called into question as she saw the real me for the first time. My descent into hell was now complete.

The only thing left to do was end it all. I began planning a way to end my life. I stopped eating and became so frail my wife feared for my health.

I came home from work one day determined to end my life. But God intervened and spared my life in a peculiar way. As I opened the door to my home, my little girl saw me. Her face lit up and she called out, "Poppie!" She ran toward me with outstretched arms. She grabbed my leg and hugged me tightly.

I reached down and embraced her. I began to cry. She loved me. How could I kill myself and leave her alone? I was the only father she knew. How selfish of me to think only of myself and my pain! I decided I would live for her, my little girl.

It was at this point that I developed the courage to call for my God. I prayed, "God, if it were just me, I'd just as soon die. But I cannot leave my daughter. I'm sorry. Please forgive me and help me once again."

I sensed that He heard my prayer. And I believed that if He heard me, He would come up with a plan for my rescue.

Living for my daughter was the most selfless thing I had ever done. It was an act of personal sacrifice. For the first time, my eyes were not on myself. They were on someone else. With this willful act of sacrifice, I moved into the realm of God-like behavior. Sacrifice called forth humility, and humility called forth repentance with subsequent forgiveness. Forgiveness ushered in hope, and hope drew my focus toward God.

My daughter was God's display of mercy at a time when I could have easily killed myself. There is no doubt that she embodied the mercy of God because mercy is feminine. And she was a little girl, God's "little feminine," in my time of need.

I decided to move out of my house to seek Him intently. Besides, I could not bear to exist under the same roof with my wife. My guilt was only matched by the magnitude of my shame.

We decided to separate temporarily while I searched for direction. I rented an apartment five minutes from our home and began earnestly seeking God. I knew this mountain of homosexuality that had plagued me for more than thirty years had to be dealt with once and for all. I could not continue ignoring it.

I knew my involvement in pornography could not go on if I wanted God's healing. But I had no idea how God was going to address this issue. It had been so long and He had never addressed it directly. Since thirteen years of age, I had been enslaved to homosexuality. I choked at the thought that at age thirty-one I would finally find the answer. My faith was weak, but I had no other recourse. I had set myself to seek Him. If God could not help me, no one could.

I prayed, "God, I know homosexuality is against You. But I am powerless against it. You have never spoken to me directly concerning it. If it is Your will that I suffer like this and there is no true freedom for me, just say the word. I'll accept my burden and go home to my family."

With that prayer, I rested from my struggle. My desires no longer mattered anymore. I would no longer bow to homosexuality. A certain peace came upon me. He was my God. I would serve Him even if it meant that I would die doing so. I decided to simply wait God out. He would speak again. I knew it.

I was still addicted to pornography. My lifelong choices had conditioned this behavior pattern. I did not know how I could win, but I was determined to do all that was within me to stop this habit.

I went to my home one day to pick up some clothing, and I saw a piece of paper lying on the bed. It appeared to have been left behind accidentally. I picked it up and noticed a Scripture reference written on it: Jeremiah 32:27. I went to my Bible and found the verse. "Behold, I am the Lord, the God of all flesh: is there anything too hard for me?" (KJV)

I looked toward heaven in wonder. God had broken His silence and spoken directly to the situation at hand. He had been listening after all.

I now dared to believe the unbelievable. God was actually going to answer my lifelong question: "What is wrong with me, how did it happen, and how do I fix it?" He was God. How could anything be too hard for him?

My whole life, I had chosen to accept things for the way they were concerning my confused feelings. Never considering true healing, I tried to work around them. Now, for the first time, I refused to accept this plague. I had a wife and a family now. I started to see that my life was no longer all about me. I had to become well if I was to be of any good to them. Surely God could heal me for them.

I acknowledged His presence with me from the day I accepted Him at eight years old. Always there, He had never left me. He had healed my stomach ache as a young child. He'd visited me in my bedroom at age sixteen and freed me from my uncle's grip. He put to flight the spirit that attacked me in my college dorm room. He promised to uphold me with the right hand of His righteousness in my time of loneliness. His silent but strong presence would not allow me to jump from the mountaintop. He strengthened my resolve to leave my first relationship. As a loving father, He corrected my foolishness when He bid me to choose between my wife and the woman at the club. He had stood by my side on my wedding day. He would not allow the spirit to kill me by bending my mind. Even in my rebellion, He had provided mercy for me in the little girl He used to steady my hand set toward suicide. He had been my strong tower even when I had forgotten him.

"If we believe not, yet he abideth faithful: he cannot deny himself" (2 Timothy 2:13 KJV). "I will never leave thee, nor forsake thee" (Hebrews 13:5 KJV). This is the fidelity of our God.

"For I am persuaded, that neither death, nor life, nor angels, nor principalities, nor powers, nor things present, nor things to come, nor height, nor depth, nor any other creature, shall be able to separate us from the love of God" (Romans 8:38—39 KJV). This is the love of our God. He loved me beyond measure.

Though I'd felt lonely my whole life, I had never really been alone. Why would God leave me in a perpetual state of misery and unhappiness? Did He not love me as much as He loved my family? Of course He did. He had shown his fidelity toward me for as long as I could remember. God would free me for one reason only: simply because He loved me.

My faith increased, and I waited with expectation. "The Lord is good unto them that wait for him, to the soul that seeketh him. It is good that a man should both hope and quietly wait for the salvation of the Lord" (Lamentations 3:25–26 KJV). "They that wait upon the Lord shall renew their strength; they shall mount up with wings as eagles; they shall run, and not be weary; and they shall walk, and not faint" (Isaiah 40:31 KJV).

My waiting proved to be the key to my eventual breakthrough. God finally broke His silence and began speaking to me on a level I had never experienced before. The next few months brought a flurry of visions, dreams, events, and even physical, earthly manifestations of His thoughts toward me.

But His words were not reserved for me alone. My wife also experienced a flurry of events, for she had her own story to tell. She was obviously distressed about all that she had learned about her husband. Her faith wavered as to whether God could fix me. But when she began to lose hope, God audibly spoke to her.

One day she was thinking about the situation and called me while I was driving to work. She told me God had spoken to her concerning me. He'd said, "He is my child. I will not forsake him."

When I heard this I was still in unbelief and had not yet spoken to God. The faithfulness in that statement was unbelievable. I had clearly left Him. Why would He choose to stay with me? At that moment, I began to understand the power of spiritual fidelity, undeserved but offered all the same. Had God behaved adulterously, I would have been left to my own ruin.

I felt a softening of my stone-cold heart. A surge of tears welled up in my eyes. I choked them down. I would not cry today.

On another occasion, she felt like giving up and decided it was over between us. She set her mind toward divorce. Then God said to her, "No. Be still."

On another occasion, as she waited on Him, He spoke to her again. "I am doing a work in him."

I was astounded by the next story she told me. She had been reading a book on spiritual warfare and began learning about spiritual attacks. Our home was large and located in a secluded subdivision. She began to feel afraid. I was not living at home at this point, so she was home alone with the children. She walked toward the window and God opened her spiritual eyes to see large beings standing around the perimeter of our home. They wore blinding white garments. Their faces were hard, stern, and warrior-like. They stood with swords raised high above their heads and their backs facing the house. It was clear what they were. These were warrior angels. God had commanded them to stand guard as a great spiritual battle was being waged against me and my family. Astonished at this sight, she went into the bedroom to lie down.

Later, my wife called me and told me about a dream she had. She said she was standing in front of our home, listening to an individual on the phone. This person was planning to go to a gay bar later that evening.

As she walked back toward the house, she saw an object in the driveway. Getting closer, she noticed it was a large snake with a big head. Its mouth was gaping toward our home, as if in an attempt to devour it. She ran into the house and picked up our younger daughter and carried her to the second floor.

As she changed her diaper, she saw hundreds of little snakes crawling around the changing table. She grabbed our daughter and placed her safely in the crib. She then noticed a knife in her hand. She began stabbing the snakes in their mouths as they lunged at her. But they would not die.

My stepdaughter would soon be home from school, so my wife steadied herself to do battle with the large snake in the driveway. Suddenly the dream ended.

On another occasion she had a dream in which she and I were speaking. I said to her, "I will kill the snake. But it will take me some time."

A few days later, I came home to visit, and as I walked into the garage I noticed a quick movement at the base of the steps. I walked closer to investigate and noticed a snake curled at the threshold of the door. I was startled. But I knew there was a connection to my wife's dreams. God was sending me a message. This was a physical manifestation of the theme in my wife's dreams.

I considered brushing the snake away but, it was in a position that made this impossible. I could not simply leave it, hoping it would go away. This was the door my family used to enter and leave the house on a regular basis. They could have been harmed by it. There was only one choice. I had to kill it.

I grabbed a shovel and struck at the base of the snake's neck, killing it instantly. I threw its carcass into the woods. When I told my wife about this, she just stared at me.

Sometime later, as I was driving, I saw a snake crossing the road as I slowly drove by. Around the same time Adam called me. In passing, he told me he'd noticed a snake in his front yard.

I knew God was trying to tell me something. So I asked Him about this. Shortly thereafter, as I sat in my apartment one day, I heard His still, small voice. "Homosexuality is a lie." I immediately understood the significance of the snakes.

In the beginning Satan came to Eve in the form of a snake. He deceived her. The snake represented the lie of homosexuality. I was not born this way and it was not my identity. I was not gay. *Gay* is a political term that describes a way of thinking about oneself. This false identity seemed a tragic choice to make. I now saw the truth: I was a psychologically wounded man whose feelings reflected his past realities. I did not want to sacrifice my family for a lie.

In regard to my wife's dreams, the lie was large and attempting to devour our home, as it had Steve's. The portion of the dream where she stabbed the snakes with a knife meant that she could not kill it. It was not her battle. I had to kill this lie in my own mind. God revealed to her His plan when I said to her in her dream, "I will kill the snake, but it will take me some time." Now I had killed it and thrown its remains into the woods. The dreams were symbolic of what God was doing spiritually. It was then that I heard God speak to me regarding the mysteries of gender.

Gender is the balance of God. Homosexuality is not spiritually or physically balanced. Physically, it is not supported by nature through replication, as is heterosexuality. In homosexual love, reproduction is not physically possible. Unlike heterosexual behavior, homosexual behavior is physically dead.

The spiritual laws mimic the physical ones. The lie of homosexuality robs us of the legacy bestowed upon us through our children. Lies do not call forth life, but only death.

It was up to me whether I would believe this truth or choose to believe a lie.

I cut off practically all communication with Steve. We ultimately took separate paths. He chose to accept the lie and become openly gay. After being married for fifteen years, with two beautiful preteen daughters, his marriage ended in divorce. In an attempt to convince me to see his darkness as light, he told me God had made him that way. But this fundamental change in his life was clearly a behavioral choice. For years he had chosen marriage, and now he was choosing something else.

On many occasions, while still not sure what to do about his marriage, Steve had asked me to let him move into my apartment. I'd told him no, that I needed to be alone to seek direction and truth. In addition, Steve had become emotionally unstable and I did not want him as a roommate.

Steve saw his divorce as an opportunity for us to live as a couple. I still felt attracted to him, but I had chosen not to have a homosexual mind-set and did not want to appear as if I had chosen him over my family. Though separated from Varee, I did not want to send her that message. Steve eventually stopped coming around.

Adam finally told his family he was gay and started another homosexual relationship. Though he and I remained platonic friends, we had little in common at this point and our connection faded away.

I was now without either friend, separated from my wife, living alone in an apartment. I had been stripped of all my crutches. It was then that God began the painful process of uncovering my love wounds.

As I sat in my apartment, quiet and alone, I watched a Christian television show. A woman told her story of addiction and how she was freed to live a life away from the control of her addictions. She spoke of the failures experienced by many who are never really free, but simply fall in and out of their particular sin in cyclical fashion.

I could understand this. I had been down my sinful road many times before.

Another woman on the show told how God revealed His love to her. She lay in bed one night, weeping. Her husband asked her what was wrong. All she could say was "He loves me, He loves me, He loves me." Somehow God got hold of her and revealed to her the mystery of His love. She grasped it at the level of the deep heart.

The first woman then paused, sat forward, looked into the camera, and said, "Now, I want you to hear this. So listen closely."

I sat forward in intense expectation.

"When you finally grasp what it means to be loved by God, your freedom will be complete."

Something broke in me. I fell to my knees and sobbed. I felt raw. God had already begun softening the stony heart that had existed within me through years of rebellion against Him. But at this moment the job was complete. I was a little boy once again, hurting and in pain. I lay there on the floor, completely broken before Him.

I examined my life from the beginning up until the present. My sin loomed large as I felt the sting of my wretchedness. I cried to God, "Lord, what is this love You are speaking to me about? What is it that I don't know about You that keeps me in this prison? Show me this love. I want to be free."

Immediately, I was taken into another vision. I was about five years of age, kneeling at the base of a large cross. The image of a man stretched wide hung there. I knew this to be Jesus. As I knelt before this cross, I covered my head, and it appeared as if I were in severe emotional pain. Then the image awakened and floated down from His position on the cross. As He descended upon me, the image changed form and became a large, billowing blanket that draped itself all around me as I knelt there, weeping. I sensed a knowledge of Him that I had never felt before. I had just experienced love. In my pain He had become "the God of all comfort, who comforts us in our troubles" (2 Corinthians 1:3).

This was the beginning of many such experiences through which God led me back in time and comforted me, as I navigated once again the painful memories of my past.

I started going to professional counseling. During one session my counselor identified a problem with my father. He asked me to expand on my relationship with him. As I talked, I was overcome with grief and began sobbing. I was immediately reminded of my plan to not speak publicly about him. I had decided this so long ago that I had almost forgotten about it. I was no longer in denial about my feelings about my dad.

Over the next six months I wrestled with the spiritual law of forgiveness concerning him. Eventually, I released him. With this decision, I moved closer to my own freedom. The releasing of my father was a gradual one, for he was at the core of my gender identity crisis as a young boy.

One morning, I awakened to a dream. I was standing in front of my father. I was about five years old and I was naked. He stood in front of me with his head hung low. He appeared to be sad about something, apparently feeling responsible for my nakedness. I walked over to him and said, "It's okay, Dad. Don't be sad. I'm not mad at you anymore."

When I awakened I searched my feelings. I felt no personal pain, but rather a softening in my heart concerning my thoughts about him. With this dream came the release of my bitterness toward father.

God then had to call me out of denial with regard to my uncle. It was odd that I had never experienced any anger toward him concerning his part in my early life. In my mind, I saw him as almost innocent. I felt it was my fault the abuse had occurred. This is a common belief in the minds of molested children.

I was still a child in the way I perceived my past in reference to my uncle's abuse. I simply felt nothing about the issue. I was numb to it. I had long since walled it away. This is an example of repression of memories. It is the way in which the immature mind deals with pain. Not knowing how to forgive sins, children merely ignore them, sometimes pushing painful experiences out of their conscious minds altogether.

One night, while lying in bed, I was startled by a distressing vision. I saw my younger daughter being molested. I watched in horror, crying, feeling helpless to save her. I then heard God speak to me. "You were someone's little boy too. But no one cried for you." Immediately, the scene changed and I saw myself.

This vision resurrected ancient memories from my subconscious mind.

I felt ill. Rage, anger, and sorrow flooded in all at once. God had effectively broken down the wall of denial I'd erected as a child against this terrible fact of my past.

My task of forgiving my uncle would be difficult since he had died many years before. I had to learn how to forgive a dead man who offered no apology for his sin against me. But we are called to forgive everyone, even if they are dead and have no ability to make amends for their sins against us. Forgiveness frees the forgiver, not necessarily the forgiven.

True forgiveness offers only; it takes nothing in return. As long as one expects some form of vindication or pity in regard to an offense, forgiveness will hide her face from you. You will forever remain in the prison of anger and bitterness through unforgiveness. This is a personal hell, chosen by those who live on the polarity of blame, the polar twin of forgiveness. Forgiveness is commanded by God for our own freedom from self-anguish. This was by far my toughest lesson.

I began to see that my life had been a long, twisted, tortuous road through a world in which I had never felt the love necessary for healthy spiritual human development. My homosexual struggles were a sign of my emotional pain and lack of personal identity and self-worth.

My gender identity crisis began with the rejection of my father when I was five years old. Had I understood true spiritual forgiveness at that point, I would have maintained an emotional connection to him and not felt the need to receive comfort from older male figures.

My neediness made me susceptible to an uncle who solidified the blow to my fragile masculine identity by molesting me in the dawn of my pubertal development. This connected sexual arousal to the male images that haunted me for years. My lack of faith in God drove me to accept a lie: that my feelings were fixed, there was no changing them, and my emotions determined my identity.

My actions then conditioned my physical responsiveness to a particular behavior pattern, leading me down the road to addiction and despair. Had God not loved me out of His feminine image of fidelity, my journey would have ended here. This is ultimately the end of all lies. We can only be freed by the truth. "He sent his word, and healed them, and delivered them from their destructions" (Psalm 107:20 KJV). "Sanctify them by the truth; your word is truth" (John 17:17).

His Word heals and His truth is His Word. Based on the Word of God, truth heals. Fight for God's truth in the heart and never believe lies. You will then be able to see clearly the things that cause you to stumble. "For the commandment is a lamp; and the law is light; and reproofs of instruction are the way of life" (Proverbs 6:23 KJV).

I returned home to my wife and family a changed man. My addiction to pornography vanished over a period of two years, in step with my spiritual growth as I dealt with the wounds of my past. The sexual images faded over time. However, on occasion I still see them. I am learning to just look at them briefly and then turn away. They no longer possess the power to torment me. The truth about them stripped them of their power over me.

Due to my years of involvement in homosexual activity, I have continued to notice some mild predilection for the old behaviors. I do not let this bother me. I now know the truth about these feelings and they are no longer overpowering. In the end, I choose my reality. These are only scars that remind me of a battle already won. I don't need to fight it again.

I believe that my freedom from this ancient foe will be a lifelong decision that I will need to make on a daily basis. My past is set in reference to neuroplasticity and development. However, truth has freed me. "Then you will know the truth, and the truth will set you free" (John 8:32).

My will now serves as the power by which my heart exerts its influence over my personal choices. Though my homosexual thoughts have diminished greatly, I no longer feel distressed when one occasionally comes to mind. Healing does not mean that God frees us from feeling anything. As we grow in the image of our God, we make choices that condition our feelings in the contrary. Freedom is progressive. We are freed as we sacrificially choose based on obedience. God-like behavior draws us closer to God and frees us based on our unique human ability to choose our realities.

In the end, God is not slack in providing us with feelings that are representative of His desires for our personal lives. To me, this is no different from thinking about eating an extra piece of cake when you have already had your fill. I simply choose moderation over gluttony.

Feelings no longer distress me. Emotions are only a mirror reflecting our past realities. Some distressing feelings are given to us when we are children, pure in heart. Others we chose for ourselves. As spiritual creatures, we are not obliged to choose our reality based on feelings alone. Spiritual maturity looks not at what we feel in self-fulfillment. It looks through the eyes of truth, and in obedience we sacrificially choose life.

God has since blessed me with a son. On the night he was conceived, I saw him in a vision given to me by God. He was an answer to my prayers. Not two months prior to his conception, I had prayed for a chance to implement the knowledge given to me that I've shared in the pages of this book. I wanted a chance to be a father to a son and have the reward of watching him grow into manhood with me at his side.

God seems to have chosen to re-create my beginnings in my son. Like me, he has a mother, two older sisters, and no other male model but a father through whom he will learn about himself as a male child created in the image of our God. Like me, he is a firstborn son.

As my daughter was God's feminine mercy in my time of need, so my son has become God's masculine provision for my personal healing. Through loving him, I have been given another chance to see myself grow up under the loving covering of a Father's watchful eyes and guidance.

I have forgiven my own father for everything, and I blame him for nothing. The weight of my sorrow is no more. I can now, in confidence, say that I truly love my dad. I endeavored to prove this by giving my son my father's name, which is also my own. This is something I thought I'd never do.

In unforgiveness, I had become foolish beyond belief. How can one hate his father and bear his name without hating himself? Today I can say confidently, "I am my father's son." We are and always will be one. Through forgiveness, God has healed me of my repressed childhood pain. I have repented of the pride that fueled the unforgiveness toward my father, thereby freeing me from the hell of self.

Forgiveness is the way of the righteous, and there are few who find it. I now proudly wear my badge of "IV" as it was intended by my father on the day of my birth. My son now takes his rightful place as the fifth generation of men in my family who bear this name. I thank God that my personal pain did not destroy such a wonderful legacy.

My war with Dad is over. I have lain down my sword. I now stand hand in hand with my father on one side and my son on the other as three generations of male image bearers, a powerful symbol of God's feminine mercy, forgiveness, and restoration.

> And the Lord shall guide thee continually, and satisfy thy soul in drought, and make fat thy bones; and thou shalt be like a watered garden, and like a spring of water, whose waters fail not. And they that shall be of thee shall build the old waste places: thou shalt raise up the foundations of many generations; and thou shalt be called, The repairer of the breach, The restorer of paths to dwell in.
>
> ISAIAH 58:11—12 KJV

---

[8]Alan Medinger, *Growth into Manhood* (Colorado Springs, CO: WaterBrook Press, 2000), 233.

Bibliography

101 Frequently Asked Questions about Homosexuality, Mike Haley (Harvest House Publishers, 2004).

The Battle for Normality, Gerard J. M. Van Den Aardweg, PhD (Ignatius Press Publishers, 1997).

The Broken Image, Leanne Payne (Baker Books Publishers, 1996).

Crisis in Masculinity, Leanne Payne (Baker Books Publishers, 1995).

Desires in Conflict, Joe Dallas (Harvest House Publishers, 1991).

Giant Killers, Dennis Jernigan (WaterBrook Press Publishers, 2005).

Growth into Manhood, Alan Medinger (WaterBrook Press Publishers, 2000).

Healing Homosexuality, Joseph Nicolosi, PhD (Jason Aronson Inc. Publishers, 1993).

The Healing Presence, Leanne Payne (Baker Books Publishers, 1995).

Homosexuality: The Use of Scientific Research in the Church's Moral Debate, Stanton L. Jones and Mark A. Yarhouse (InterVarsity Press Publishers, 2000).

Homosexuality and the Politics of Truth, Jeffrey Satinover, MD (Baker Books Publishers, 1996).

Legislating Immorality, George Grant and Mark A. Horne (Thomas Nelson Inc. Publishers, 1984).

Pursuing Sexual Wholeness, Andrew Comiskey (Charisma House Publishers, 1989).

Reparative Therapy of Male Homosexuality, Joseph Nicolosi, PhD (Jason Aronson Inc. Publishers, 1991).

Setting Love in Order, Mario Bergner (Baker Books Publishers, 1995).

Sheep in Wolves' Clothing, Valerie J. McIntyre (Baker Books Publishers, 1999).

Strength in Weakness, Andrew Comiskey (InterVarsity Press Publishers, 2003).

A Strong Delusion, Joe Dallas (Harvest House Publishers, 1996).

That Kind Can Never Change! Can They? Victor J. Adamson (Huntington House Publishers, 2000).

The Truth about Homosexuality, John F. Harvey, OSFS (Ignatius Press Publishers, 1996).

Wild at Heart, John Eldredge (Nelson Books Publishers, 2001).